BON JOVI

The Story

BON JOVI

The Story

BRYAN REESMAN

STERLING

New York

STERLING
New York

An Imprint of Sterling Publishing Co., Inc.
1166 Avenue of the Americas
New York. NY 10016

ISBN 978-1-4549-2104-2

Distributed in Canada by Sterling Publishing Co., Inc.
c/o Canadian Manda Group, 664 Annette Street
Toronto, Ontario, Canada M6S 2C8
Distributed in the United Kingdom by GMC Distribution Services
Castle Place, 166 High Street, Lewes, East Sussex, England BN7 1XU

For information about custom editions, special sales,
and premium and corporate purchases, please contact Sterling
Special Sales at 800-805-5489 or specialsales@sterlingpublishing.com.

Manufactured in China

2 4 6 8 10 9 7 5 3 1

www.sterlingpublishing.com

Designed by Paul Palmer-Edwards
Picture credits are on p. 205

CONTENTS

SHEDDING THEIR SKIN

AFTER ACHIEVING FAME AND NOTORIETY, CAN ONE ESCAPE THE PAST? AFTER BECOMING SO INGRAINED IN OUR COLLECTIVE BRAINS, CAN A SUPERSTAR BAND REINVENT ITSELF AND MOVE ON? CAN THE BAND MEMBERS GROW UP? WILL WE LET THEM?

In the case of Bon Jovi, the answer is a resounding yes.

Since the band broke through to worldwide fame in the late 1980s with the mega-selling *Slippery When Wet*, which celebrates its thirtieth anniversary in 2016, the hard-rocking quintet from New Jersey have been an easy target for naysayers. They have faced the condescension of critics and the scorn of some metal fans who felt that they took their genre in a pop direction. Their hard hooks and pretty boy looks certainly made them a commercial force to be reckoned with early on, and the fact that they could write catchy tunes and put on a big show endeared them to the fans who flocked to their concerts again and again.

It is certainly true that so many rock bands that were massive in the 1980s, particularly a lot of poodle rockers from the Sunset Strip and Bon Jovi's home state, have never returned to the same level of prominence as they had during their heyday. Bon Jovi avoided that curse by altering its image and music in keeping with the times. While the 1990s were a quieter, if still successful, period for the group, their international resurgence in 2000 with the album *Crush* reinvigorated their career in a way that no one expected. Since that time their worldwide tours have grossed massive amounts of cash, increasingly so to the point that their tour for *The Circle* in 2010 grossed $201 million globally, making it the third-highest-grossing concert tour in the world according to Pollstar, and the *Because We Can tour* raked in just shy of $260 million to become the Number 1 tour in the world in 2013 and the fifteenth-highest-grossing tour of all time. They have sold over 130 million records worldwide and performed more than 2,700 concerts in over fifty countries for more than thirty-four million fans. Some of this may come as a surprise even to people who still follow the band, and it might be a bit of a shock to those who wrote them off a couple of decades ago. But as Frank Sinatra, another famous New Jersey icon, once declared, "The best revenge is massive success." If that is the case, then Bon Jovi has achieved that with a vengeance.

Although, anger has not been the driving factor here, Jon Bon Jovi has confessed to having a chip on his shoulder that keeps him motivated. Since he was a teenager, he sought the spotlight,

and once he grabbed it, never relinquished it. Charging forth from New Jersey, the indefatigable frontman and songwriter practically willed himself to become a rock star. Luckily he found four equally ambitious bandmates who helped him achieve his dreams and fulfill them beyond what he might imagine. (Fun fact: Jon Bon Jovi, Richie Sambora, David Bryan, and Tico Torres were all delivered by the same doctor in Perth Amboy, New Jersey. How's that for kismet?)

Throughout the course of their career, principal songwriters Jon Bon Jovi and guitarist Richie Sambora (along with notable collaborators Desmond Child, Billy Falcon, and John Shanks) have amassed a repertoire extolling the virtues of hope, faith in a better future, facing down hard times, and the desire to make a better life for oneself.

Their signature song "Livin' on a Prayer" was a simple ode to love and faith in the face of difficult odds. It was not necessarily offering a way out; the solution was for its protagonists Tommy and Gina to stick things out together, to weather the bad times, to treasure their love, and hopefully build a better life down the line. In a world that has become increasingly obsessed with being number one, this was not some pipe dream about winning the lottery or turning the tide. It was about riding out turbulent seas. That theme has reemerged numerous times over the course of their thirty-three-year recording career, manifesting itself in other hits such as "Keep the Faith," "It's My Life," and "We Weren't Born to Follow."

Still, how does a band who became known for a signature glam look and booming anthems like "Bad Medicine," "Raise Your Hands," and "Lay Your Hands on Me"—a cocksure combination that launched a million hair bands—manage to survive the Decade of Decadence and find relevancy within the continually changing tides of musical styles and trends? In a word: maturity.

That maturity came with a price, notably the near disintegration of the band following the grueling, epic world tour in support of their multiplatinum album *New Jersey*—the successful

❰❰ I USED TO WATCH THEM ON THE SIDE OF THE STAGE AND THOUGHT, 'MAN, THIS IS A GREAT BAND.' THEIR PARTICULAR BRAND OF ROCK 'N' ROLL WAS UNIQUE, OBVIOUSLY WITH JON'S VOICE WHICH IS VERY FULL OF CHARACTER AND THEN JUST THE OVERALL MUSICIANSHIP. I'VE ALWAYS FELT IT'S VERY DIFFICULT TO MAKE THAT KIND OF MUSIC IN THAT IT'S OBVIOUSLY NOT METAL, IT'S NOT HARD ROCK, BUT IT'S A VERY STRONG ROCK 'N' ROLL PERFORMANCE. SO THE ACTUAL MUSICIANSHIP IN THAT RESPECT HAS TO BE REALLY TOP CLASS. SOME METAL BANDS RELY ON VOLUME TO GET THEIR MESSAGE ACROSS. THAT WAS NEVER THE CASE WITH BON JOVI. ❱❱

Rob Halford, singer for Judas Priest, January 2016

sequel to the multimillion-selling *Slippery When Wet*. But from the smoldering ashes of that intense conflagration arose a wiser, more musically sophisticated group who graduated from writing about girls, partying, and simple empowerment anthems into crafting songs that dived into deeper emotions, social issues, and the wisdom that comes with age. With the occasional rousing rocker tossed in for good measure.

Like any veteran rock band, Bon Jovi have had their share of ups and downs, hits and misses, periods of furious activity and much-needed breaks. As of spring 2016, the slightly reduced core of the so-called Jersey Syndicate—Jon Bon Jovi, keyboardist David Bryan, drummer Tico Torres, and longtime bassist Hugh McDonald—were at work on their first studio album of fresh material in three years. This album would witness the studio debut of new guitarist Phil X—a younger musician taking the place of Richie Sambora, who unexpectedly departed from the group early into their extensive 2013 world tour. As during other periods of upheaval in their history, this was a new test for the band. And if history has proven anything, it is that their frontman thrives on hard work and rising to meet any challenge.

When I set out on writing this book, I was already impressed with how Bon Jovi have managed to stay hugely popular over time. Few classic rock bands have been able to maintain that kind of pace and following. But I was blown away by how deep their history goes, the connections they have to other artists, and how many projects they have been involved with.

Ultimately, Bon Jovi is a better band than many people think. Jon is a first-class frontman. Richie is a consummate guitarist. They have written some classic songs and worked with some talented collaborators. Highly skilled keyboardist David and dynamic drummer Tico are vastly underrated as players. And their "unofficial" replacement for original member Alec John Such, bassist Hugh McDonald, can play his ass off. (By the way, can he be made an official member now?)

If you are looking for a muckraking exposé, this isn't it. This is a tome about music, with some behind the scenes drama that set the stage for many of the hits they wrote and recorded. So, let's head back to where it all began, in a modest town in New Jersey where a young man dreamed of becoming a rock star, unaware of the adventure that he and his brothers in music were about to embark on.

Once upon a time, not so long ago . . .

OPPOSITE: Jon Bon Jovi front and center as his band performs at London's O₂ Arena on the sixth of a twelve-night stand during *The Circle* tour, June 17, 2010.

INTRODUCTION

I

POUNDING THE PAVEMENT

1975—1981

THE TRIED AND OFTEN TRUE CLICHÉ OF THE RAGS-TO-RICHES ROCK STAR HAS BEEN CITED COUNTLESS TIMES, BUT IN THE CASE OF JON BON JOVI ONE WONDERS IF HE WAS BORN READY-MADE TO TAKE THE WORLD BY STORM. JOHN FRANCIS BONGIOVI JR. WAS BORN ON MARCH 2, 1962, IN PERTH AMBOY, NEW JERSEY, TO JOHN SR., A MARINE TURNED HAIRDRESSER, AND CAROL, A MARINE TURNED PLAYBOY BUNNY TURNED FLORIST. SHIRKING THE STEREOTYPE OF STRICT MILITARY PARENTS AS THEY RAISED THEIR SON IN NEARBY SAYREVILLE, THE COUPLE ENCOURAGED JOHN TO FOLLOW HIS ARTISTIC DREAMS. AND HIS DREAMS WERE HUGE.

His initial aspirations to play guitar at age seven were stifled by an apathetic music instructor, leaving John to follow other pursuits like dirt biking and football. But by the age of thirteen, he immersed himself in popular music and, seeking to emulate his idols, he picked up that six-stringed instrument once more and attempted to teach himself to play. He soon needed guidance and sought out a family neighbor and musician named Al Parinello, who was in a local club band.

"I asked him for lessons," Jon Bon Jovi told Lisa Russell of *People* magazine in November 1986. "He said, 'What for?' I said, 'Chicks, what d'ya think?' He said, 'Good enough.'" Despite not being a teacher, Parinello offered to train the fledgling rocker—he first taught him to play "House of the Rising Sun" by the Animals—but clamped down on him fast. When Jon had not learned the song after the first three lessons, he told him not to waste his time. Jon got the point and became disciplined and studious, absorbing whatever he was given. Parinello taught the novice guitarist the basics and the discipline that has served him well throughout his lifelong career. To this day, Jon has the initials AP chiseled on a black acoustic guitar that he uses in live shows. Parinello passed away in 1995.

By the fall of 1976, Jon (who still went by his birth name John—the spelling was formally changed when Bon Jovi was formed seven years later) began attending St. Joe's Metuchen,

PAGE 10: A young Jon Bon Jovi practicing his heartthrob pose.

a private Catholic all-boys high school on the Metuchen-Edison town lines. There he met guitarist Wil Hercek in a classroom in 1978. Jon had brought in his guitar. The two talked music. Wil recalls in our interview for this biography that Jon was forming a band to play a 1950s-style dance that Al Parinello had arranged. Although the gig fell through, the group—then consisting of Jon, Wil, and bassist Steve Pretti—began formulating bigger plans while rehearsing in the singer's basement. (Jon had previously assembled the Raze for a high school talent show.)

Sometime in 1978, Jon transferred to Sayreville War Memorial High School (where he met friend and future Skid Row guitarist Dave "Snake" Sabo) and continued with the band, which was modeled after Southside Johnny and the Asbury Jukes. Wil, who lived in Perth Amboy, was originally the one member from out-of-town. Over the next year, the group began accruing members, rehearsing in the basement of drummer Mark Scimeca, and morphing into a ten-piece, horn-heavy ensemble as people found their place in the band, now called the Atlantic City Expressway. Lead guitarist Bill Frank and keyboardist David Bryan Rashbaum (now better known as simply David Bryan) later became key members.

The Atlantic City Expressway played covers of J. Geils Band, Bruce Springsteen, and the Asbury Jukes—all artists that Jon idolized, particularly the latter. They learned the songs by playing along with the albums or to the radio. "We did a whole arrangement of [Springsteen's] 'Kitty's Back'," says Hercek. "I had a skip in my record, so we played the skip. That always used to blow me away."

The Atlantic City Expressway's first gig was playing Borough Park Hall in Sayreville, in the fall of 1978, followed by various college and pub gigs during 1979. On October 6, 1979, the group played their first big venue, Sayreville War Memorial High School. "We conned the Board of Education in Sayreville into letting us use the auditorium," recalls Frank in our

interview. "Basically all we wanted to do was play on a big stage, so I created an event with this guy Steve Medlin, this 'Save the Whales' concert. We were the opening act for a band called Whisper, which was a popular band in town. They did classic rock—Clapton, Traffic, and Uriah Heep, that kind of stuff. We really treated it like a concert. There were T-shirts. I actually still have one. We had all our friends who were ushers. The local department store that I worked at was the sponsor of the show."

The group's following grew as they frequently played clubs in New Jersey including Dodd's 80's, Brothers III, Big Man's West (the club of Springsteen saxophonist Clarence Clemons), and even one gig at famed NYC punk club CBGB. ("That didn't go so well," notes Frank.) Their first and most important venue was the Fast Lane in Asbury Park, where they later landed a weekly Wednesday gig after Jon arranged an audition with club manager Jimmy Giantonio. Hercek recalls that when they walked into the club for the first time, "T. Roth and Another Pretty Face was playing. In the band, which I didn't know at the time, was Tico Torres. Jon didn't know who Tico was either. Nobody knew anyone. But this guy Roth used to play originals. He was really great, a little bit Bowie-ish with some eye makeup."

Jon's band began to build a local fanbase. On January 9, 1980, the newly minted star Bruce Springsteen jumped onstage to sing with the teenage singer and his fledgling outfit. "When Bruce went onstage, I thought Jon was going to have a fucking stroke," laughs Jack Ponti, an eighties hard-rock songwriter and producer who later became a R&B artist manager and then indie label CEO, who was one of Jon's early bandmates.

ABOVE: A vintage shot of Southside Johnny and the Asbury Jukes, local icons and personal heroes to Jon Bon Jovi. Johnny and Jon have since become good friends, with Jon borrowing guitarist Bobby Bandiera for a couple of Bon Jovi tours.

❝ I'D GO TO HIGH SCHOOL AND SAY, 'WHAT DID YOU DO LAST NIGHT?' AND KIDS WOULD SAY, 'I WATCHED *DALLAS.* WHAT'D YOU DO?' I'D SAY, 'I JAMMED WITH BRUCE SPRINGSTEEN, THAT'S WHAT I DID.' ❞

Jon Bon Jovi to Lisa Russell, *People* magazine, November 24, 1986

F & M Productions Presents

SAVE
THE WHALES

WITH

WHISPER

AND THE

ATLANTIC CITY
EXPRESSWAY

SAYREVILLE WAR MEMORIAL
HIGH SCHOOL AUDITORIUM

OCT. 6, 1979

7 p.m.

Tickets Available at our Sponsors' Location

Greenfield's Dept. Store, 95 Main St., Sayreville, N.J.

Platter Puss Record Shop, Rt. 9 Sayerwood Shopping Center, Old Bridge, N.J.

Donation $4.00

Make checks payable to F & M Productions Save The Whales

"T" Shirts & Refreshments will be sold

All Proceeds Will Go To Save The Whales Inc.

15

"We were playing at the Fast Lane doing the [Springsteen] song 'Promised Land'," Frank also recounts. "Jon coaxed him with his hand and Bruce came up. The place went crazy." The guitarist recalls that Bruce often came to their shows and had been backstage to encourage them a few times.

Even though Jon often showed up to high school completely exhausted from late-night bar gigs with the band, his parents knew there was a creative spark there, and they

ABOVE LEFT: A replica poster of the "Save the Whales" concert that was the Atlantic City Expressway's first major gig in 1979. This signed poster was created for the twenty-fifth anniversary show on October 15, 2004. David Bryan later replaced then-keyboardist Jack Gadowski.

ABOVE RIGHT: A 1979 advertisement in the *Aquarian Arts Weekly* for the New Jersey club the Fast Lane, where the Atlantic City Expressway played many headlining gigs, including the one listed.

supported his rock star desires. According to Laura Giantonio (the photographer and DJ at the Fast Lane and now former wife of Jimmy), Jon's mother, Carol, regularly attended his shows and looked out for him.

While the Atlantic City Expressway was doing well, Jon was seeking new horizons. By April 1980, Jon had decided to depart from the group. "I think the kicker was when we got a new drummer, Jeff Kinder, who was an older guy, maybe four or five years older than us," says Hercek. "He played like Max Weinberg and had that simple set, and he became the leader of the band. I think Jon soured on that a little bit, although Jimmy Giantonio was encouraging him to get out [and do things]."

Fortuitous circumstances emerged when Jimmy told Jack Ponti, frontman and songwriter for rock band the Rest, that he should check out Jon in concert. Jack recollects that upon meeting him after one of his gigs with the Atlantic City Expressway, Jon insistently asked him for help with his demo. "He had never written a song in his life," says Ponti. "One thing led to another and he wedged his way into the band." Seeing the effect Jon had on girls outside of a cover band, Jack thought it best to let him stay onboard.

Jon and Jack seemed like kindred musical spirits. In an interview with local New Jersey writer Bill Chemerka, Jack declared that they were in it for the money and leaving the artsy rock to those who were not. He was being facetious, but his sentiments would be echoed by Jon after he broke big in talking about representing youth culture and doing things for

BUILDING THE EXPRESSWAY

ONCE JON TRANSFERRED TO SAYREVILLE WAR MEMORIAL HIGH SCHOOL IN THE FALL OF 1978, HE BEGAN AGGRESSIVELY BUILDING UP A STRONG BAND.

"Jon started just recruiting people from marching band at Sayreville," recalls guitarist Wil Hercek. (Jon played trumpet for a short while in his high school marching band.) "He reached out to the sax player, Rick Cyr, who reached out to the Durrua brothers, Bill and Ken. Ken played trombone and Bill played trumpet. They were both excellent musicians. Then we got another trumpet, it was crazy. We had horn players going in and out, but that was pretty much the basis of the band."

Lead guitarist Bill Frank (whose stage name later became Billy Pontiac) was recruited into the band because he ordered fried chicken and answered the door with his guitar on. The delivery boy for Frank's fried chicken was Expressway bassist Steve Pretti, and he knew who Bill was—"I was as much of a legend as you could be in Sayreville, New Jersey at that time," Frank tells me—and soon he was invited to jam with the band, whose members were about three to four years younger than the twenty-year-old Frank.

Despite having different musical tastes—he liked country rock like the Outlaws and the Allman Brothers, whereas they were into Bruce, the Jukes, and classic R&B—he joined their ranks. "They seemed like nice kids, and Jon quite frankly was impressive vocally even then," he remembers. They already had a few gigs lined up. It has been said that a great performer acts as though they are performing in an arena even if they are playing to an audience of only twenty people, and Jon soon became known for his electric stage presence in whatever group he fronted.

The final piece of the Expressway puzzle was keyboardist David Bryan Rashbaum, who attended J. P. Stevens High School in nearby Edison with Jon's cousin, Joseph Bongiovi. Joseph told David that Jon needed a keyboard player. David had been studying piano with Emery Hack (who was then bandleader for the NBC Orchestra) from the age of seven. ("He was a wonderful teacher," Bryan told Scott Iwasaki of the Utah newspaper, *Deseret News* in April 2001. "Emery was like the David Copperfield of music. He'd just play and do these things that were amazing.") The young David Bryan Rashbaum had chops. He also had a big Hammond organ, a Fender Rhodes, and a big van (which was a huge plus). Intrigued by the musical prospect, he went over the bridge to Sayreville and brought his gear to Jon's basement where the band had been rehearsing. "It was a ten-piece band—five-piece horn section, five-piece rhythm section—that was it. That is where it started. I was sixteen-and-a-half [and] had my driver's permit. It was a Springsteen/Jukes cover band with originals. I knew 'We Are Having a Party' and 'Born To Run' and I knew I could play classical, so I figured I could figure out any other song they threw at me. They asked if I knew all these songs by Springsteen and the Jukes, and I said, 'Of course I do.' They asked what key it was in. I [thought if] I could figure out Chopin I could figure out Bruce," David Bryan told Tobi Drucker Tesoriero of *Living In Monmouth Magazine/Living In Media*, on June 30, 2009.

They soon became bandmates. And so it began.

DODD'S 80'S

...It Was Meant To Be!

Wed Mar 12
Casablanca Recording Artists

SAM THE BAND
MARK MUSCATELLO

Thurs, Fri & Sat Mar 13, 14 & 15
Performing The Sounds Of The Asbury Jukes & Bruce Springsteen

ATLANTIC CITY
EXPRESSWAY

College Night
Sun Mar 16

St. Patrick's Day
Blow Out!!!

Beginning
At 4 p.m.!!!

Join Us For Our Outrageous St. Patrick's Day Party
Featuring Non Stop Music By N.J.'s 3 Top Bands!

ATLANTIC CITY EXPRESSWAY
HOLME
THE SHAYDS

DODD'S 80'S

10 N. CENTER ST. ORANGE, N.J. / RIGHT OFF RT. 280
201-678-2270

❝ WE USED TO FIGHT CONSTANTLY ABOUT PLAYING. DURING THOSE BILLY SQUIER SESSIONS WE WORKED THE GRAVEYARD SHIFT BECAUSE WE COULDN'T AFFORD THE REAL STUDIO TIME. WE WOULD START AT 11 AT NIGHT AND END AT 7 IN THE MORNING. IT WAS JUST HORRIFYING. WE WOULD GO DOWN TO JERSEY AT 9:30 OR 10 O'CLOCK IN THE MORNING. [ONE TIME] OUR MANAGER CALLED AND SAID, 'I GOT YOU A GIG TO PLAY AT HEAT TONIGHT.' I SAID, 'FUCK THAT.' JON SAID, 'WE'RE PLAYING IT! WE'RE PLAYING IT!' 'DUDE, WE DIDN'T EVEN SLEEP.' 'WE'LL SLEEP NOW!' ❞

Jack Ponti, Jon's former bandmate and songwriting collaborator, January 2016

the fans. They were unapologetic populists, and both men would move on to great success in different ways. From around April 1980 through to the end of that year, Jon, Jack, guitarist/keyboardist Mick Seeley, bassist Walt Lukas, and drummer Tommy Swift kept rocking with the Rest, a band whose sound was akin to the Knack. The quartet played the Fast Lane and other Jersey clubs and continued their push toward success. Jack likened the Fast Lane to Los Angeles's famed Whisky a Go Go—plenty of major artists came through its doors, including the Police, Pat Benatar, and Meat Loaf. "We played the Fast Lane twice a week," recalls Ponti. "We rehearsed at the Fast Lane." Jack adds that Fast Lane owner Phil DeAngelo and the club's booking agent and manager Jim Giantonio were the Rest's managers.

While the Rest was rocking local stages, Jon was smitten with a beautiful classmate named Dorothea Hurley, who originally had a boyfriend—Jon's friend Bobby. But after Bobby joined the navy, Jon made his move. During their senior year, Jon courted Dorothea and the two shared a strong bond and a similar rebellious spirit. Jack recalls seeing Dorothea at some of the Rest gigs.

Jack remembers Jon writing his first song around this time, called "Bobby's Girl." "I still have the lyrics in his handwriting here somewhere," he says. "He came to practice one day and said, 'Check this out, I wrote this for Dorothea.' It wasn't bad, it just wasn't great." It was not going to set the music world afire, but it was a start. The two-minute tune was allegedly a declaration of love to her.

The band dynamic was shifting, however. "[Jim] didn't feel Jack was a good front man," relates Laura Giantonio when we speak. "I thought Jack was a genius. He was great onstage. Jack was the one that was killer." In contrast, she notes, Jon was "very laid back and very sweet." She admits she thought Jack was going to become the big rock star, but Jon had an ardent fanbase.

"All the girls in high school went crazy over him," says Giantonio. "That was it. I was in my twenties and I didn't see it because he was seventeen years old. It was the high school girls. He married his high school sweetheart." Not all audiences loved them, however. "When the Rest opened up for Southside Johnny"—at the Freehold Raceway on July 4, 1980—"people were booing like crazy and throwing things."

OPPOSITE LEFT: Fast Lane photographer and DJ Laura Giantonio (on left) in her group the Fabulous Perms, who performed primarily at the Fast Lane and who knew "Runaway" songwriter George Karak. They recorded a four-song EP on Wrong Records in 1981, produced by John Ogle and featuring future the Rest's guitarist Mick Seeley.

ABOVE RIGHT: A newspaper ad for the Rest featuring singer John Bongiovi (bottom left) and guitarist/songwriter Jack Ponti (bottom right). The group created a buzz but ultimately could not land a record deal.

During 1980, the Rest recorded two sets of demos featuring songs penned by Ponti. The first demo tape was produced by Southside Johnny and Garry Tallent at House of Music in West Orange, New Jersey (where Meat Loaf did *Bat Out of Hell*), and included the songs "Telephone Line" and "Pretty Girls." The second demo was produced by Billy Squier, before he broke big with "The Stroke," at RPM in New York City and featured the tunes "Other Side of the Night" and "Call a Different Lady." "I borrowed $1,500 from my mother to pay for that demo," recalls Giantonio.

At a young age, Jon was already exhibiting the drive, determination, and passion that would lead to his success. He was also ballsy. Later on, between 1981 and 1982, Aerosmith were in the studio recording *Rock in a Hard Place* at Power Station, and singer Steven Tyler was in rehab. As Tyler recounted on *The Howard Stern Show* in January 2016, the young Bongiovi allegedly chastised and warned the Aerosmith frontman that they could miss out on their opportunity to reclaim their former glory.

Jack Ponti also recalls Jon being very savvy about the business side of things: "He had convinced our managers to give Jon and I a salary, and that was the last thing I was thinking about," he admits. "The rest of the band didn't get that, so that was a secret between Jon and I. He and I had a weekly salary."

> ◀◀ AT THAT TIME, THE MOVIE *10* WAS PRETTY POPULAR SO DOROTHEA—OR DACKY AS EVERYBODY CALLED HER—HAD HAIR LIKE BO DEREK'S WITH BRAIDS AND BEADS. DOROTHEA WAS JUST A WONDERFUL, WONDERFUL GIRL. I THINK SHE'S ALWAYS BEEN JON'S ROCK. SHE WAS THEN AND OBVIOUSLY CONTINUES TO BE. ▶▶

Jack Ponti, January 2016

During his time in the Rest, Jon graduated from high school and, wanting to keep his rock star dreams alive, soon secured a job at Power Station, the famed Manhattan recording studio owned by his second cousin, producer and mixer, Tony Bongiovi. Tony had made his name engineering Motown albums for the likes of Stevie Wonder and Diana Ross and the Supremes, as well as rock acts such as Dr. John and Jimi Hendrix. He founded the studio in 1977.

Jon took on gofer duties at Power Station—sweeping floors, fetching coffee, running errands—basically doing anything that anyone needed doing. It did not hurt that music icons like Mick Jagger, Carly Simon, and David Bowie passed through Power Station's hallowed halls—the teenage Bongiovi was in his element. He would later become an assistant engineer on some projects. "If my memory hasn't gotten really foggy, I think Jon was an assistant on some of the gigs," keyboardist Larry Fast tells me. "He was damn good and was a nice guy and very energetic. I got to know him just casually through the staff people." The situation with the Rest, however, was not going that well by the end of 1980.

"I broke the Rest up because I felt there was no place to go," says Ponti. "We just kept hitting the wall. I remember one time Jon and I were up at the RCA office with Nancy Jeffries, and she was jumping off her chair like we were the next Beatles. 'This is the greatest thing I've ever seen, it's the greatest thing I've ever heard!' She was going to sign us, so Jon and I spent the weekend on the Jersey Shore celebrating. And she called on Monday and said, 'No, we're going to pass.' I just felt there was nothing else to do."

Minor fortune shined on the ambitious singer in 1980 when Tony booked Jon's first recorded performance—lead vocal on "R2D2 We Wish You a Merry Christmas" for the *Star Wars Christmas Album*. It was not going to be the big break he needed, but he earned his first recording credit.

In 1981, Jon wanted to try his hand leading his own all-originals band, so he formed the short-lived Johnny and the Lechers with guitarists Bill Frank and Wil Hercek, bassist Ed Horne, and drummer Jim McGrath. Bill recalls that the two-guitar band's music was in a poppier vein like the Romantics. They recorded a few demos of original tunes at Power Station including "Don't You Believe Him," "Don't You Keep Wondering," and "Head over Heels."

ABOVE: Jon (left) and Jack (right) rocking out on the stage of the Fast Lane in Asbury Park, New Jersey, on July 18, 1980.

"ONE DAY WE REHEARSED IN THE CITY AND WENT BACK TO THE POWER STATION. WE PULLED UP [IN A CAB] AND GOT OUT, AND THIS LIMO PULLS UP IN BACK OF US AND IN BACK OF THEM ANOTHER CAR. THESE GUYS GET OUT OF THE LIMO, AND THE GUYS IN BACK OF THEM GET OUT. THEY'RE PAPARAZZI. THE GUYS IN THE LIMO WERE CHARLIE WATTS AND MICK JAGGER. THEY WERE DOING *TATTOO YOU*. I REMEMBER CHARLIE HAD A SIX-PACK OF HEINEKEN. WE WERE LIKE, 'HOLY SHIT! IT'S THE STONES!' WE WALK UP AND SAY HI, AND MICK COMES OVER AND PUTS ONE ARM AROUND ME AND ONE ARM AROUND JON, AND SAYS, 'THIS IS MY NEW BAND, THE FROGS.' THOSE PAPARAZZI HAVE THAT PHOTO. THEY PROBABLY DON'T KNOW THAT IN THAT PICTURE WAS THE FUTURE ROCK STAR JON BON JOVI. "

Bill Frank, guitarist and Jon's former bandmate, February 2016

The quintet soon morphed into John Bongiovi and the Wild Ones with a slant towards eighties rock, which Bill was not as enamored with. He says he was "a bluesy, country-ish guy. I was weaned on Eric Clapton and Robin Trower, so that's my style. I wasn't Eddie Van Halen." The group gigged out a lot and played on local Jersey cable television staple the *Uncle Floyd Show*. They wrote and (late at night) demoed songs including "Somewhere Loving You," "Maybe Tomorrow," "Don't Leave Me Tonight," and "Who Said It Would Last Forever?" Bill says the initial Wild Ones lineup included him, Jon, bassist Danny Sky, keyboardist Tom Pyle, and drummer Charlie Mills. Bassist Mick Seeley, drummer Tim Mount, and Jon's old friend David Rashbaum on keyboards were eventually enlisted into the group. Saxophonist Rick Cyr recorded with them.

In April 1981, Jon and Jack collaborated again and came up with the song "Shot Through the Heart" that later emerged on Bon Jovi's debut album. The singer had been working on original material with his new band, Bill Frank says that between the Lechers and the Wild Ones they recorded about fifteen demos. (Twenty tunes, including an instrumental version of "Runaway" and three tunes Jon wrote with Jim Pooles, surfaced many years later on the bootleg CD *The Power Station Years: The Unreleased Recordings*.) On bus rides from Sayreville to the city and back, Jon tirelessly wrote lyrics for songs, even penning them on his bedroom wall.

Musicians at Power Station offered him encouragement, including a young rocker named Aldo Nova. Jon and Aldo struck up a friendship, later leading to Aldo providing some guitar and background vocals on Bon Jovi's eponymous debut. But despite being in the thick of the music industry, Jon's demos were falling on deaf ears as record companies rejected his offerings.

That ever-elusive record deal remained the key to igniting the young Bongiovi's career, and Jon needed to find that one great song that would set him free from the pack.

THE ALDO NOVA CONNECTION

THROUGHOUT ALL OF THE MAJOR STORIES THAT HAVE BEEN WRITTEN ABOUT BON JOVI, ONE NAME THAT RARELY POPS UP IS ALDO NOVA—THE CANADIAN SINGER, SONGWRITER, AND GUITARIST WHO BEFRIENDED JON BEFORE HE BROKE BIG.

The dancing keyboard line and muscular riffing of Aldo's hit single "Fantasy" propelled his self-titled debut album to Number 8 on the Billboard Top 200 Albums chart, going gold at the time and amassing sales of over two million copies by 1989. The pop-metal blueprint that Aldo laid down on his first three albums between 1982 and 1985 was echoed in Bon Jovi's debut album, and it makes sense given their history.

Aldo Nova recalled to Joe Nichols on *The Performers* television show in Vancouver in 1992 his first meeting with Jon Bon Jovi at the Power Station, "I bump into this kid by the coffee machine, and he was working there as an assistant engineer, so we started talking." Aldo recognized a fellow singer-songwriter and they struck up a friendship. Jon checked out his album in progress and loved it, and Aldo caught one of his shows. "Then my record took off like a bullet, and when Jon needed somebody to play on his first album he called me up. I played guitar on 'Runaway' and keyboards and sang background on the whole first album. That's how we got to work together ten years ago."

When comparing the debut Aldo Nova and Bon Jovi efforts, the influence is apparent. The mixture of hard guitars and poppy keyboards matched with anthemic hooks must not have been lost on Jon. Aldo's third album, *Twitch*, in 1985, even featured a talk-box-laced anthem called "Lay Your Love on Me" which could have comfortably fitted on Bon Jovi's third album *Slippery When Wet* in 1986. While his pre-fame bandmates do not see the correlation with the singer-songwriters that Jon worshipped, Derek Shulman, who later signed the band to PolyGram, also believes that Aldo was an influence. "Yes, he was, because Aldo was in the studio at the same time as Jon and they became very close friends," concurs Shulman when we chat. "Aldo was a friend of Tony Bongiovi. He actually lived [in Tony's apartment] above the studio. Tony loved Aldo."

Aldo's career stalled after 1985—and he became dormant for six years to wait out the expiration of a label contract he disliked—but Jon and Aldo stayed friends and reconnected when the latter played guitar and keyboards on his superstar friend's first solo album, *Blaze of Glory*, a tie-in to the 1990 western movie *Young Guns II*, which featured two of its songs. The album's dramatic title track won Bon Jovi a Golden Globe Award.

Jon then helped produce and co-wrote Aldo Nova's 1991 comeback album, *Blood on the Bricks*, which was released on Bon Jovi's own Jambco label. In a way, things had come full circle with Jon's bluesy, anthemic songwriting style adding an extra kick to Aldo's new music. They later collaborated again on the Bon Jovi solo song "Mister Big Time" for the *Armageddon* movie soundtrack tie-in in 1998.

Aldo Nova has penned hit songs for the likes of Celine Dion, Faith Hill, and Clay Aiken. Aldo won a Grammy Award in 1996 as producer for Celine Dion's *Falling into You*, which won Album of the Year. He co-wrote the Latin Grammy-nominated song "Aqui" on the Chilean rock group La Ley's album *Uno*, which won a Grammy for best Latin Rock/Alternative Album. He also co-wrote Clay Aiken's Number 1 hit "This Is the Night" with Chris Braide and Gary Burr—it was the best-selling American single of 2003, according to *Billboard* magazine.

The Canadian songwriter and performer has played live again in recent years, and founded a new company called Viral Entertainment in 2014.

OPPOSITE: A signature Aldo Nova pose (left) from a 1981 concert. His sound would pre-date and later influence the first wave of pop-metal bands, a movement that Bon Jovi helped popularize with *Slippery When Wet* six years later.

22

❝ I MET JON WORKING AT POWER STATION. . . . WE LOOKED SIMILAR. HE LOOKED LIKE A SINGER-SONGWRITER, SO I ASKED, 'WHAT DO YOU DO?' HE SAID, 'I'M A SINGER-SONGWRITER.' AND I SAID, 'I'M MIXING MY RECORD IN STUDIO A, WHY DON'T YOU COME IN AND LISTEN TO IT?' HE CAME IN AND LISTENED TO MY ALBUM AND SAID, 'THIS STUFF IS GREAT, WHY DON'T YOU COME OVER TO THE RITZ TONIGHT, I'M PLAYING THERE.' SO I WATCHED HIM AND WE GOT TO BE PRETTY GOOD PALS. ❞

Aldo Nova to Joe Nichols, *The Performers* television show, 1992

II

POWERING UP

1982—1983

ENTER GEORGE KARAK TO THE SAGA IN 1982.

Unlike the cover artists dominating the Jersey scene, George Karak says he always performed original tunes. His first group, Tony Romeo and the Sinners, played "mostly R&B à la Motown . . . with a splash of the British invasion of the 1960s," says Karak during our interview. The group was active from 1972 until 1982, at which time he and some of the members formed an eighties AOR (album-oriented rock) band called Intruder that released two albums of catchy tunes in Europe and Japan via British-based Escape Records. Intruder lasted for a decade.

While performing with his side project George Karak and the Streethearts in 1982, George was approached by the young Bongiovi after a gig at the Fast Lane. George had seen Jon's group once or twice and thought they were good. He did not know that Jon's second cousin owned Power Station.

"He walked up to me," recalls Karak, "and, I remember this clear as day, said: 'I really like the way you write music. Do you want to write some songs together?' That's how it all started. He said, 'Do you want to meet me at the Power Station? I want you to meet Tony and Lance [Quinn, who later produced Bon Jovi's first two records.]' I went up there and strummed out a bunch of songs for them. They picked some songs, and asked, 'Do you mind if we record them?' I go, 'No, go ahead.' I had nothing to lose because I was twenty or twenty-one years old. So they did. . . . We worked on 'Runaway' a little bit over at his [Jon's] house in Sayreville. I had a lot of the song written, but he changed a couple of lines in the second verse. I pretty much wrote the whole thing, but I was a fair guy. I told Jon, 'Whether you write two lines in a song or I write two lines in a song, we'll split down the middle.' That's just the way it was back then. It didn't really matter. We were all young and wanted to get something going. It was an agreement."

Jack Ponti and Laura Giantonio attest that George had essentially written an earlier version of the song prior to meeting Jon. Funnily enough, George Karak (and Tony Bongiovi, for that matter) hardly ever gets mentioned in major televison profiles on Bon Jovi, the man or the band. In June 1982, Jon recorded some demos at Power Station produced by Lance Quinn. George recalls that three of his songs were recorded, all of which he says he had written or co-written: "Talking in Your Sleep," "All Talk and No Action," and the epic "Runaway," the iconic song that

PAGE 24: A young Richie Sambora solos during Bon Jovi's opening slot for ZZ Top at Madison Square Garden, September 24, 1983. It was their first major arena gig.

ABOVE LEFT: George Karak, the co-writer of "Runaway," fronting George Karak and the Streethearts at the Fast Lane, Asbury Park, New Jersey, circa 1981–82.

ABOVE INSET: The "Runaway" vinyl seven-inch single from back in the days of turntables.

ABOVE RIGHT: An ad for a headlining show for Scandal with John Bongiovi as support in 1982. The young frontman appeared in two Scandal videos prior to their major label deal.

would launch the career of Bon Jovi the band. Recorded by a one-time group dubbed the All Star Review, "Runaway" featured future Bon Jovi bassist Hugh McDonald.

"Jon was sweeping floors and making coffee at the time and he had this song," McDonald said to Scott Iwasaki of the Utah newspaper, the *Park Record* on September 13, 2013. "The producer [Lance Quinn] was in a band with one of my friends [and future Bon Jovi sound engineer] Obie O'Brien who I had known from Philadelphia." One morning, Quinn called McDonald at 2am to do a session. "At that time, Bruce Springsteen was in one of the studios, so they asked his keyboardist Roy Bittan to play on the song. In one of the other rooms, John Waite was doing his first album, so they asked [drummer] Frankie LaRocka and [guitarist] Timmy Pierce to play. And that was the band." Once "Runaway" was cut, John Bongiovi and the Wild Ones started performing it at their gigs.

Then twenty-three years old, Tim Pierce recalls the group recording at least six and possibly eight songs over a few days, including "Runaway" and "Talking in Your Sleep," which he soloed on. "I met Jon when I was doing a John Waite record, and of course Jon was living upstairs [in Tony's apartment]," Pierce tells me. "He liked my playing. He befriended me, and then when it became time to do his demos he flew me out a little early. I was already heading to New York on other stuff." The session pros did not have long to learn the songs. Tim does not recall recording late at night but does recall Aldo Nova being there.

"THE KID I KNEW WAS A GOOD KID. HE JUST WANTED TO MAKE IT. HE HAD THE CHARISMA, HE HAD THE LOOKS, HE JUST NEEDED THE SONGS. THAT'S ALL IT CAME DOWN TO. HE HAD THE WHOLE PACKAGE, HE HAD THE VOICE. OF ALL THE BANDS THAT PLAYED IN OUR AREA IN THAT AGE GROUP, IF ANYBODY WAS GOING TO MAKE IT WAS GOING TO BE HIM. "

George Karak, co-writer of "Runaway," January 2016

"Jon was absolutely laser focused on being a rock star, and I was pretty impressed by that fact," says Pierce. "I had never really seen anybody that determined and that clear at that age." He recalls that Jon and David later came out to Los Angeles "to find musicians to put together because I think he was tired of his bandmates. Maybe he was looking for a guitar player, but he was trying not to rely on his neighborhood dudes. I do remember that." Tim and Jon crossed paths a decade later when the former performed a solo on a Christmas song that Jon and Don Felder contributed to for the 1992 compilation album *A Very Special Christmas 2*.

Interestingly, sometime in the first half of 1982, Jon appeared as a guitarist in two promo videos for Scandal—"Love's Got a Line on You" and "Goodbye to You" (in which he lurks in the background)—that were shot to help get that band a record deal. Their debut EP came out that year. Some people think he was in the band briefly, but the more likely possibility is that he was filling in for another guitarist for the shoot(s). Certainly Bill Frank has no recollection of Jon being in Scandal.

However, Bill notes that Jon did get him auditions for both Scandal and Billy Squier. While neither gig panned out, the gestures were welcome. "I guess Jon thought pretty highly of me, and I always appreciated that," says Frank. "If he could get me a gig that was going to get me what I wanted, he did the legwork for me."

Around late 1982, frustrated by lack of label interest, Jon visited a burgeoning Long Island radio station called WAPP to try to get airplay for "Runaway," and was encouraged to enter the song into their Rock to Riches contest at the behest of a DJ there. The winners would be included on their ten-song *New York Rocks 1983* compilation of local talent released by the station. The song made the final cut, and when the collection was released, became its runaway hit, growing in popularity in select American markets because WAPP was part of the Doubleday chain of radio stations.

Some of those same labels that had originally said "no" to the young Bongiovi before were now proclaiming "yes," as A&R men sought out the fresh new face with the hot tune.

The way in which the classic lineup of Bon Jovi was formed began with David Bryan Rashbaum, who had been accepted to the prestigious Juilliard School of Music. Jon lured his friend away from a life of classical music with the promise of fulfilling their rock 'n' roll fantasies. David had toiled hard to get into Juilliard after beginning college at Rutgers

OPPOSITE: Trini Lopez (center) and Jon's second cousin Tony Bongiovi (right) at Power Station Studios on November 10, 1978. Tony gave Jon an important break by allowing him to work and record at Power Station before he had a record deal.

University, but he took a chance on Jon again and recommended two older musicians to form their rhythm section—bassist Alec John Such and Cuban-American drummer Tico Torres, who had played together previously in the band Phantom's Opera. Such had been playing in Richie Sambora's band, Message, and Tico was playing for Frankie and the Knockouts, whose first two albums had broken the Top 50 in the United States and who had scored the Top 10 hit "Sweetheart" in 1981. Tico had joined the Knockouts after their big hit was released; now he was taking a chance on an unproven group after getting a good vibe from Jon, despite the latter being a few years younger than him.

The last piece of the puzzle was the guitarist position. Dave Sabo filled the six-string slot for a short time, playing live with the band as they capitalized on their burgeoning popularity, but then a hotshot young axeman—a cocky former bandmate of Such with plenty of live experience—pestered Jon to join the band after witnessing a couple of their gigs. He was told by the singer to learn the group's material.

▌▌ QUITE HONESTLY, I THINK IF THAT PARTNERSHIP HAD NEVER OCCURRED IT WOULD'VE BEEN A WHOLE DIFFERENT STORY. RICHIE WAS SO IMPORTANT. IF MCCARTNEY NEVER MET LENNON, WOULD THEY HAVE BEEN A SUPERSTAR BAND OR JUST A GOOD BAND? ▌▌

Bill Frank, February 2016

Jon arrived late to the subsequent rehearsal to hear young Richie Sambora jamming harmoniously with his bandmates and immediately gave him the gig.

Bon Jovi the band was born.

Some time after the WAPP compilation was released, Jon landed a record deal. Jack says he sent the song to Atlantic Records and solicited interest from them. However, Jon had been

> **"WHEN I MET WITH JON [AND HIS PARENTS] BACK IN THE DAY—AND HIS MOM AND DAD WERE VERY INSTRUMENTAL IN HIS LIFE AND STILL ARE—HE WANTED IT SO BADLY IT HURT. THAT WAS PART OF WHY HE MADE IT. HE WANTED THAT FAME AND FORTUNE AND TO BE THE BIGGEST ROCK ARTIST IN THE WORLD, BUT HE DIDN'T KNOW IN WHAT FORM IT WAS GOING TO BE. WE WALKED THROUGH THE KINDS OF BANDS THAT HE WANTED TO BE. DID HE WANT TO BE LIKE A REX SMITH OR A VAN HALEN? IF IT WAS ROCK, HE HAD TO GO OUT [AND TOUR]."**

Derek Shulman, music industry mogul, February 2016

approached by Mercury Records, who ultimately won out thanks to the enthusiasm and enticing offer from Derek Shulman, an A&R representative at the time who would later ascend to the position of senior vice president of A&R for Mercury and who had previously fronted seventies progressive rock band Gentle Giant.

An interesting fact about the band was confirmed by Sambora in a 2009 band profile on *60 Minutes*: only Jon's name has ever been on the contracts and the members are all technically hired guns. "Jon was signed to the label," confirms Shulman in our interview. "He didn't want the band signed to the label, which gave away, even back in the day when he was that young, how he felt about himself. However, he was quite generous to the band. The band was certainly not shaking cups outside Times Square."

The offer to Bon Jovi did not come about simply due to the song. Derek was first introduced to "Runaway" by a Philadelphia attorney named Arthur Mann, who played him the tune and said he knew it was going on the WAPP compilation. He played him other demos as well. Meanwhile, Jon had been grooming his band for success when an intrigued Derek went to see them in early 1983.

"'Snake' Sabo had gone and they had Richie in the band," recalls Shulman. "I saw them at the Copacabana actually. I brought along a couple of people from the company as I was reporting [to them], and they [the band] did a showcase for me. To tell you the truth, they weren't that good. They played five songs. Jon's attraction and his appeal and drive were incredible." Derek adds that he told Jon he felt bassist Alec John Such was a liability to the band. "His stage presence was very good, but to be perfectly honest his playing was not that great. I have to tip my hat to Jon. Not on a personal level, but as far as playing was concerned, I told Jon that he should not be in the band when he first started, and Jon had loyalty to Alec."

Despite his initial misgivings about the group, Derek knew something special was happening. He felt that Richie was "a fantastic addition to what I had originally heard. And we developed it." He signed them to Mercury by early spring 1983. Derek suggested a name change as well, from the ethnic John Bongiovi to the more rock star-ish Jon Bon Jovi. He adds that Jon wanted to call the band Desire, but he thought that was a horrific moniker.

RIGHT: Bon Jovi's A&R guru Derek Shulman back in 1975, when he was fronting progressive rock icons Gentle Giant. Shulman successfully transitioned from art rock to the major label world and signed popular bands including Cinderella, Dream Theater, Pantera, and Nickelback.

"To be perfectly frank, I stole the idea from Van Halen and gave it to Jon, and Jon thought it was a great idea," admits Shulman. "So Jon Bon Jovi and Bon Jovi the band. Van Halen had the same situation, and now I'm owning up to it for the first time." Looking back on the band's history now, one can sense an early identity crisis in that the band and label were trying to figure out what Bon Jovi would be.

Having met Doc McGhee when he was managing Pat Travers, Derek remembered how effective he was at getting what he needed wherever he went. Now Doc was managing Mötley Crüe and seemed like a good match for Bon Jovi. Derek introduced Doc to Jon, the two clicked, and a fruitful partnership was born.

Just prior to that, Bon Jovi got another great break when they opened for ZZ Top at Madison Square Garden on September 24, 1983. "Managers started courting him, and one manager was John Scher, who at that time was a massive concert promoter," explains Jack Ponti. "In order to look like he was cool and groovy, John Scher in his courting process let them open up for ZZ Top."

"Nobody knew who the hell they were," admits veteran rock photographer Eddie Malluk, who shot the show. "ZZ Top are a different type of band, and especially back then nobody cared about opening bands. By the time the set was finished, they [Bon Jovi] won some people over, but it wasn't their type of audience. There weren't that many women there. There was that kind of gruffy, bluesy Southern rock thing—the ZZ Top thing. It was a good break for them because there was a lot of press there because it's New York, so it got coverage."

Having gelled through their live shows, the group then cranked out their self-titled album around the early fall of 1983 at Power Station, with a release set for January 1984. Some of the songs had been demoed and worked out previously and were ready to record. Lance Quinn produced the album that would set the stage for their mainstream arrival.

It was one small step for Bon Jovi, but the giant leap was yet to come.

THE ORIGINS OF SAMBORA

BEFORE HE JOINED THE RANKS OF BON JOVI, RICHIE SAMBORA WAS A RISING STAR IN HIS OWN RIGHT.

Born Richard Stephen Sambora on July 11, 1959, in Perth Amboy, New Jersey, the talented six-string slinger had music in his blood from the start. An only child raised in a very modest home in Woodbridge, he picked up the accordion at age seven—he was allegedly able to play "Strangers in the Night" by ear after one lesson. He took up the guitar at age thirteen, teaching himself to play along to blues-rock icons like Jimi Hendrix, Eric Clapton, and Jeff Beck. Three years older than Jon, Richie attended Kean University of New Jersey for two years after high school, but he always knew he wanted to be a rocker. His first break came in an unexpected way in 1979. Longtime friend Bruce Stephen Foster (who played piano on the first KISS album and had released his first American album *After the Show* on Millennium-Casablanca Records in 1977) had a trio gig with bassist/producer Tommy Marolda, who got food poisoning one night. "The club [Charlie's Uncle] only held sixty or seventy people," Foster tells me. "I said, 'Is there a bass player in the house? Mine is retching in the parking lot.' Richie and two of his friends were sitting at a table three feet from the front of the stage, and Richie laughed and said, 'Hey, I'm a guitar player. I've never even held a bass before, but I'll give it a shot.'"

While he fumbled on bass—he did not even know how to tune it, notes Bruce—Richie's good humor and desire to redeem himself on guitar led to Bruce bringing him back as a guest the next week. During "Kansas City," pleased with Richie's rhythm playing, Bruce offered to let him solo. "I was expecting him to do this whole hotdog thing, and instead he hit the toggle switch to the lead position on his guitar and hit one note and bent it up, and it sounded like Yo-Yo Ma playing a cello," recalls Foster. "It was so beautiful, the one note had such precision and eloquence, that I turned to him before he hit the second note and said, 'You're in the band.' I gave him his first job and hired him on one note."

Richie was now in a band that had a weekly gig at Charlie's Uncle, so they were able to play under a different name every week. "It was just going out and having fun, but the club owners knew who we were and it didn't matter what we called ourselves," Marolda recalls to me, laughing. "We went out and played whenever I could or they could. It was a bunch of musicians that would just go and have fun, all based around Bruce." They treated their music with a sense of humor, although the fan name that stuck was Shark Frenzy because of how they looked when they rocked out onstage. It was this moniker that Bruce used when he reissued their demos on CD in 2004. Shark Frenzy existed between late 1978 and early 1981, and Bruce says their major influences included the Clash, the Rolling Stones, and the Beatles.

"I was doing most of the lead singing with Shark Frenzy, and Richie sang a couple of the songs," says Foster. "The first songs Richie ever wrote were with Shark Frenzy. One is called ' A Good Life'." Richie's vocals in Shark Frenzy are striking for how rich and mature they sound for someone so young. Marolda says Richie also contributed to his recording project, the Toms.

PAGES 32-33: Jon and Richie strut their stuff at Madison Square Garden as they open for ZZ Top on September 24, 1983. The group was still cultivating their image and stage show, but they were already working hard to win over audiences.

OPPOSITE: Richie is all smiles during a mid-1980s concert. The agile guitarist brought musical chops, songwriting skills, and an infectious energy to the band.

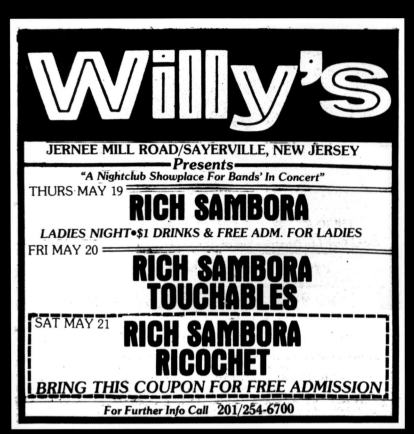

In 1980, Richie was also part of the rock band Mercy, which included singer Dean Fasano. The quintet had a short-lived and unfruitful deal with Led Zeppelin's Swan Song label, which floundered following the death of Zeppelin drummer John Bonham that year. After Mercy, Dean and Richie formed Message, which included bassist Alec John Such. Bruce likens them to Styx: "A little more highly evolved rock, much more polished and organized," he says. "I listened to that Message album and just thought there are great songs on it, and if they had gotten a record deal somehow I really thought it would've been a classic album."

Message did release the six-song album *Lessons* in 1982 on Richie's own label, Dream Disc Records (Bruce contributed organ and keyboards), but it did not make a very big ripple, although they did open some shows for Joe Cocker. At the time, the guitarist was also playing with local New Jersey act Duke Williams and the Extremes, who had a deal with Capricorn Records. He occasionally performed solo in New Jersey as Rich Sambora.

The timeline for Richie's arrival in Bon Jovi is around early 1983. The guitarist got a golden opportunity to audition as Ace Frehley's replacement for the band KISS in Los Angeles. "So Alec went to work for Jon." Sambora explained to Nicholas Barber in an interview for the *Independent on Sunday* on January 7, 1995. "We kept in touch, and when I got back he said: 'Why don't you come down and see us play?'" (Sometime around then, Richie also got a bit part in the John Travolta movie *Stayin' Alive* as the rhythm guitarist for the band of Cynthia Rhodes's character, which included members of Shark Frenzy and Frank Stallone's band Valentine.) Following his return from Los Angeles, Richie witnessed a couple of Jon's shows, was impressed, and pestered their charismatic frontman to audition. He boldly felt he was the band's missing link, but Jon was not immediately convinced. "I'd gone to a Ray Charles show one night, and then I went to see these guys open for Joe Cocker, so I was bluesed out that night," Bon Jovi commented in the same interview. "I remember thinking that Alec was great, but I didn't think Richie was right for what I was doing." But Richie convinced Jon to let him try out, recalling that "[Jon] came in, listened to it, and said: 'You're hired.'"

"Immediately, I thought he was very smart, a great frontman, a very talented musician," added Richie about Jon. "He's a very dedicated guy, very focused. He always had a good heart, always took care of the people in the band. It's very important for everybody to take care of each other, especially the bandleader, and Jon's clearly the bandleader. He looked out for us."

ABOVE LEFT: Advertisement for a three-night gig for Rich Sambora in Jon's hometown of Sayreville, New Jersey. Oddly enough, their paths did not cross until 1982.

ABOVE RIGHT: Richie at the dedication of Richie Sambora Way, which leads to Woodbridge High School in his hometown of Woodbridge, New Jersey, November 24, 2009.

OPPOSITE: Richie lets rip at the band's Castle Donington appearance in England, August 1987.

III

FROM JERSEY TO JAPAN

1984—1985

LABEL DEAL? CHECK. SOLID DEBUT ALBUM? CHECK. STRIKING FIRST VIDEO? KIND OF.

The first Bon Jovi clip from their self-titled debut, for the lead single "Runaway," intercut band performances with a bare-bones storyline about a hot schoolgirl whose parents feared her because she had pyrokinetic powers akin to the girl in Stephen King's *Firestarter*. All the action took place inside a foggy studio amid post-apocalyptic rubble, and the young lady was ultimately transformed into a groupie. Although not a work of art, the low-budget video showcased the sheer energy of the group. With the exception of Jon, none of the band members performed on the single, and Richie was miming a Tim Pierce solo. But they sold it like they owned it.

While these days they rarely play anything live from their first album other than "Runaway," their eponymous debut was a good first effort that tied in with the end of a golden era of North American hard rock that eschewed a no-frills approach embellished by good performances and genuine emotion. Bands like Y&T, Dokken, Black 'n' Blue, and Keel fell into this category, although Bon Jovi benefited greatly from having the classically trained keyboardist David Rashbaum (who would use his middle name, Bryan, in place of his surname for professional purposes by their second album). The sound was hard-edged but radio friendly, and it echoed the crossover sounds of Aldo Nova.

"Runaway" became a Top 40 Billboard hit, peaking at Number 39 on the Hot 100 singles chart, and remains a concert staple. The band's lush, catchy rendition of the melancholic "She Don't Know Me," a sixties pop-rock number written by Mark Avsec of Donnie Iris and the Cruisers fame, reached Number 48 on the Hot 100. It is the only track in the band's official studio catalog not written or co-written by any member.

Bon Jovi's debut was quite different than the "optimism in the face of adversity" anthems that become their trademark during the late 1980s. While performed with gusto, most of this original batch of tunes were melancholic odes to heartbreak, deception, longing, and love gone bad—typical fodder for young rockers of the day—and many of the titles reflected that: "Shot Through the Heart," "Roulette," "Burning for Love," and "Come Back." The album ended with the upbeat stomper "Get Ready," which made for a good concert anthem. Their youthful lyrical perspective certainly resonated with their growing fanbase.

PAGE 38: Alec John Such launches into a dramatic pose and makes a pink bass look badass during the group's opening slot for Scorpions at Madison Square Garden on June 6, 1984.

OPPOSITE: A 1984 ad for Bon Jovi's debut album. The vinyl cover wrapped around to the back to display Jon's four bandmates on the other side of the street. Jon's place as bandleader was made clear from the outset. Band manager Doc McGhee's last name is accidentally misspelled.

BON JOVI ALBUM

Release dates: January 21, 1984 (US); April 16, 1984 (UK)
Recording studio: Power Station, New York City
Producers: Tony Bongiovi, Lance Quinn
Engineers: Larry Alexander, Jeff Hendrickson, John Bengelshmy
Singles: "Runaway," "She Don't Know Me," "Burning for Love,"
"Breakout"
Top chart positions: 43 (US, *Billboard*), 71 (UK)

Side one
1. "Runaway" (Jon Bon Jovi, George Karak; 3:50)
2. "Roulette" (Bon Jovi, Richie Sambora; 4:41)
3. "She Don't Know Me" (Mark Avsec; 4:02)
4. "Shot Through the Heart" (Bon Jovi, Jack Ponti; 4:25)
5. "Love Lies" (Bon Jovi, David Rashbaum; 4:09)
Side two
1. "Breakout" (Bon Jovi, Rashbaum; 5:23)
2. "Burning for Love" (Bon Jovi, Sambora; 3:53)
3. "Come Back" (Bon Jovi, Sambora; 3:58)
4. "Get Ready" (Bon Jovi, Sambora; 4:08)

The group itself was an interesting mix of personalities, but they meshed well. Being the oldest, Tico seemed like the more responsible father figure, although he and Alec were the ones who would occasionally be seen with cigarettes in their mouths in promo photos. In contrast, Jon from all accounts was straight-edged and very career focused. All of them, Richie and David included, came off as fun and playful on stage and with the media.

Now that they had released an album, it was time to prove themselves on stage.

After spending years slogging it out in clubs, Jon and his bandmates got some amazing touring opportunities right out of the gate, especially when one considers that they were a brand new group. The quintet was off and running with a North American tour with Scorpions (who were promoting their massively successful *Love at First Sting* album), which gave them two months to get used to coliseums and civic centers in American cities like New York, Charleston, Memphis, and Jacksonville. "I think it was a good tour because you got the same kind of core audience," notes photographer Eddie Malluk. "The Scorpions had gone commercial, so you had AOR fans there."

> ❝ WE SENT JON AND THE BAND ON THE ROAD ALL OVER THE WORLD. WE TOLD THEM TO WATCH THESE BANDS AND SEE WHAT THEY DO, AND THEY DID AND THEY LEARNED. THEY BECAME INCREDIBLE ON THEIR OWN. ❞
>
> **Derek Shulman**, February 2016

Bon Jovi were astute students. "Doc McGhee used to send them out every night when we played and said, 'Just copy the Scorpions. That's all you have to do'," says former Scorpions drummer Herman Rarebell with a laugh. "They were standing every night on the side of the stage [and watching us]."

In August 1984, Bon Jovi did an eight-day-long tour of Japan, where they were already becoming stars. Upon their return to the West, they picked up another important opening slot on a six-week-long European trek with KISS, who were riding high on the platinum success of *Animalize*, their second album without their trademark makeup.

After the lengthy touring of 1984, Bon Jovi did not rest. Jon told MTV in the summer that he had been informed by the label that they would begin work on their next release on

November 10. The tour ended November 6. So they quickly jumped into writing and recording their second album, *7800° Fahrenheit*. Given that the main hit from their previous album was not performed by the band, and its second single was someone else's song, this was their chance to prove themselves with all-original material.

For several weeks between January and March 1985, the Jersey quintet assembled their sophomore effort at the Warehouse, a new studio in Philadelphia where Lita Ford had recently recorded. Jon and Richie would soon become the core writing partners in the group, but David contributed to three tunes ("Only Lonely," "The Hardest Part Is the Night," and "(I Don't Wanna Fall) to the Fire") and Tico to one ("Secret Dreams"). David's songs in particular had a larger-than-life emotional quality that helped them stand out, which makes it a bit surprising that he has since played less of a part in the songwriting department.

Returning producer Lance Quinn generated a slightly harder vibe than their debut effort, and the guitar and keyboard sounds kept pace with the times. The lyrics were slowly maturing as well. Although a harder album than its predecessor, *7800° Fahrenheit* continued to tell tales of romance gone awry, relationships falling apart, as well as life on the road—all personal themes the band members knew intimately. They had gone through their share of heartache. By the end of their first year of touring, Jon's four-year relationship with Dorothea had ended and Tico's marriage had disintegrated. Tico owned a home and Alec was also married, while the rest of the band lived with their parents. The long periods of separation, and perhaps the financial stress, were tearing some relationships apart, and the strain and sadness surfaced in several songs.

"In that era of that second album, everyone lost their girlfriends, wives, whatever," Tico Torres said on *Inside the Actor's Studio* in October 2009. He recalls how they were stuck with each other's misery, "We were all living together." They were also making little money. The group shared a poorly heated apartment with little furniture and minimal food in the fridge. Richie reportedly did solo gigs and Tico did session work to make ends meet. In spite of these issues, their fun camaraderie prevailed and the band became musically tighter and more assured than ever. They evidently channeled their frustrations into song. Two of the album's three videos, "Only Lonely" and "Silent Night," reflected that emotional turbulence.

❝THE AUDIENCE REACTED VERY WELL TO THEM. . . . WHEN I SAW THE FIRST FOUR TO FIVE ROWS WITH A LOT OF GIRLS, I TURNED TO RUDY [SCHENKER] AND SAID, 'THIS GUY'S GOING TO BE A BIG STAR, WATCH OUT.' THAT'S EXACTLY WHAT HAPPENED. FOR ME, HE WAS ALWAYS THE BRAD PITT OF THE ROCK 'N' ROLL BUSINESS. ❞

Herman Rarebell, Scorpions drummer 1977–1996, February 2016

BIG IN JAPAN

IT HAS ALWAYS BEEN A ROCK CLICHÉ TO SAY THAT YOUR BAND IS BIG OVERSEAS, BUT BACK IN 1984, BON JOVI WERE ALREADY STARS IN THE LAND OF THE RISING SUN BEFORE THEY WERE WIDELY RECOGNIZED IN THEIR HOMELAND.

They embarked on the four-date Super Rock '84 stadium tour of Japan, which took place between August 4 and 12. The package also included Canadian underdogs Anvil, future superstars Whitesnake, breakthrough stars Scorpions, and headliners the Michael Schenker Group. The show at Tokyo's Seibu Stadium was captured on a video release by Toho—the studio widely associated with the *Godzilla* franchise.

The recorded performance of their half-hour Tokyo set proves that the Jersey rockers were tight and in sync. Bon Jovi's energy and passion immediately connected with audiences, and Jon was already proving himself to be a worthy frontman. The quintet clearly enjoyed playing on stage and would do whatever they could to keep the audience pumped up. David Bryan even jumped out from behind his keyboards to get the fans clapping harder. Extended jams were used to keep the audience energy level high. They were going to win people over no matter what.

On the flip side, the experience of ardent Japanese fandom no doubt caught the band by surprise. This was during a period when it was typical to find hundreds of fans waiting for Western rock bands outside their hotels. In an interview with MTV's Mark Goodman after they returned to the United States in spring 1984, Jon recalled how the members of Bon Jovi would have to dress incognito because up to 1,000 kids would be waiting for them outside their hotel. They jokingly called their bodyguard "Now." (As in, "I need you now.") The man evidently knew what to say to the exuberant fans to keep them at bay.

The crazed fan phenomenon was not exclusive to Bon Jovi, but their looks certainly helped. Western rock bands had been experiencing such insane reverence since at least the late 1970s, as Judas Priest frontman Rob Halford recalls to me. "They didn't have anything like that in Japan, plain and simple," he says of the hard rock and metal of the time. "They didn't have those kinds of bands playing that kind of music, looking that kind of way, putting on those kinds of shows. The Japanese have always been very respectful and hungry for that kind of Western style of music."

Halford remembers that at the first hotel that Priest checked into in the late 1970s, the manager respectfully asked them to leave because it was mobbed with fans. "Girls running up and down the hallway screaming and banging [on the doors]," he elaborates. "It was very un-Japanese. The Japanese were like, 'Is this a good idea? This is completely tangent to our respectful, polite, nonintrusive type of way of living.' So for us to bring that into Japan at that time was extraordinary. It was pretty much the same wherever we went. That was for a bunch of metalheads. I can only imagine that Jon and the boys had Beatlemania."

For Bon Jovi, Japan would be the first of many countries to fall in love with the band. Being stars in that country would be an ego and morale booster for them, and it was just the beginning of their international fame.

PHOTOS BY WILLIAM HAMES

——リッチーのシンボル・マークは、星形ですね。
どうして？
リッチー：オレの一生のシンボルだって、決めてる
んでね。まだ子供の頃、部屋に星形を貼りまくった
ものさ。そうすると、外に居るみたいに錯覚するか
らね。ちょうどギターを始めた頃、ライヴ・ハウス
で見たギタリストが、ネックの所に、スターを付け
てるのを見て、かっこいいと思ってき。それ以来、
何かというと、スターを付けてるんだ。

PHOTOS BY MIHO KATO

BON JOVI 共同インタビュー
9.24 BON JOVI DAY/JAPAN
REPORTED·YUKO KATO

メンバーが、アレクとディヴを中心に、冗談の応酬
を続けるが、ジョンは黙々とハーモニカを吹く♪

需要と要望だけは無限大、というボン・ジョヴィ
しかし、日本では特別に共同インタビューという
で、実現しました。（イギリスでは、それはとい
った）それだけを見ても、それはとてもフ
を受け入れ、初めからボン・ジョ
らなりの律儀な姿勢がわかります。また意識的
か、それとも偶然なのか、この1年以上に渡
リッペリー・ツアーは、日本でスタートし
に、アメリカ東部とカナダをミニ・ツアー
前座としてであり、いわゆるウォーミング
・ツアーである。）

だからね。日本へは、このツアーが始まった時に来
て、それ以来、我々は13ヵ月がかりで14ヵ国、300
万人の前でやって、得てきた経験を生かしたコンサ
...と思う。（めでたい♥）

86年にスタートしたワールド・ツアーのラストを
飾る日本公演、その直前まで全米を繰り返し、繰り
返し踊るボン・ジョヴィのツアーを訪ねた。そして
ートが終わり、会場を去るメンバーの群れ。コンサ
るファンの群れ。（世界中どこでも、同じなんだ）ひ
とり、ひとり、何かメンバーの車を追い駆け
も、何でも欲しくてたまらないのだ。視線で
すがるファンを避けるメンバーなのだ。そして、追い
は、まるで違っていた。高価な衣装、3年前見た時と
デザイナーが、特にメンバーおのおのの個性に合わ
せて作ったもの。これは、専任
ぶプライベート・ジェット…もう、よして欲しい。
いていない。なんてブルのは、次の公演地に彼らに合
他ならぬメンバーもわかっているそうだ。
活の変化は：少なくとも、その一部は、彼ら自身が
望んだものではないはずなんだけどな。

BON JOVI
BON JOVI INTERVIEW USA発
© ARLETT VEREECKE

何を犠牲にしても、
オレにはロックン・ロール・オンリー

PHOTO BY PETER ANDERSON

世界のボン・ジョヴィになった途端、ガリガリ亡者
例えば、単なるロック・バンドのボン・ジョヴィか
ら、一躍「世界
金もうけしか頭にないガリガリ亡者共が、突然
のボン・ジョヴィ」になった彼らから、一躍「世界
た。連中は、メンバーの気持ちなんぞ
し、何枚Tシャツが売れるか？とか、おかまいな
ンフは増刷した方がいいんだろうか？とか、ツアー・パ
考えている。みんな、バンドの成功の分け前が欲し
いのだ。

ジョン：だけど、オレには文句を言う資格はないな。
やりたいことをやって、成功できて…ネ。
だろう？昔は、レコーディング・スタジオの床を
せっせと願いていたんだぜ。知ってん
ジオに出入りさえできりゃ。どういう形でも、スタ
な気がしてさ。その夢が実現したなんて、奇跡に近
いんじゃない？（笑）
——ついでに、まともな休みは、まるでナシのジプ
シー生活？

雑誌の表紙になるのは、今でもうれしい。全部切り
取って、額に入れて壁にかけてあるんだ。

ジョン：ライヴをやるのが、オレの快楽なんだから。
あんな気持ちイイことってないよ。
オレ達のために、遠くから旅してくれたんだ
は、長い間かかって、遠くから旅してきたキッズの大半
で、オレのコンサートで、チケット代を貯めてきたキッズの大半
とっても自慢に思ってるし、めいっぱい燃えるんだ。
り、疲れたりしないよ。それだけには、飽きた
雑誌を、はじからはしまで読みつくしたり、14才
ク雑誌を、はじめから、内緒でクラブに出入りしたり。（笑）それ
の頃から、内緒でクラブに出入りしたり。（笑）それ

——ジョンの体はあまり丈夫じゃ
が、体にいいことを、何かやって
体が弱いわけじゃないが、アレル
ていて、毎日何種類もの薬を飲ん
は医師が同行しているそうだ。）
ジョン：ビッグ・マックを食べて
飲むのが、健康の秘けつさ。（笑）
——それだけ？
ジョン：（苦笑して）オレ元気
ング・ストーン紙に載った記事
アーが、とても長かっ
状態が悪いんじゃないかって
しはまるで大丈夫さ。（通訳が
手に持ったハーモニカを吹き
——誰か、ソロでレコードを
か？
ジョン：（うなるように）No
——前に、映画『フット・ル
そうですが、今回のアルバム
も出演依頼が殺到していた
ズ』の名前が出ると、「また
る。）
ジョン：今度『フット・ルー
（一冗談）昔、映画の話は
ったし、今もやる気はない
ロックン・ロールだけ

予定開始時刻をかなり過ぎて、ボン・ジョ
ってくると、前列のカメラマンが一斉にフ
をたく。遅れた理由というのが、また傑作
かり前に到着したボン・ジョヴィ一行、そ
って、同じホテルにマイケル・ジャクソン
ていることを知って、同宿のよしみじゃな
ことで、突然会いに出かけたのでした。
ない上、面識もないので、"さぁマイケル
行こうぜ♥"というボン・ジョヴィも、
の皮の厚さですけど、蟻ももらさぬ警備
が相手だけに、顔パス同然。そこは全
威力ですね。で、天下の対面が実現し
ボン・ジョヴィを迎えたマイケルも
良くて、つい話し込んでるうちに、遅れ
か。で、何を話したかっていうと、大
いことばっかりで、終始、"日本人っ
くて、親切だなぁ。"と、そればっかり
プライベートな密会なので、写真は
ジョヴィのスタッフが、1枚でもあれ
ついてました。（1枚でもあれば…
もめ息）

インタビューは、各誌記者が日本語
間に入った通訳が、それと、各を
スムーズに入りました。

7800° FAHRENHEIT ALBUM

Release dates: April 12, 1985 (US); April 29, 1985 (UK)
Recording studio: Warehouse Studios in Philadelphia, Pennsylvania
Producer: Lance Quinn
Engineers: Larry Alexander, Obie O'Brien, Bill Scheniman
Singles: "Only Lonely," "In and Out of Love," "The Price of Love (Japan)," "The Hardest Part Is the Night (UK)," "Silent Night"
Top chart positions: 37 (US, *Billboard*), 28 (UK)

Side one
1. "In and Out of Love" (Jon Bon Jovi; 4:25)
2. "The Price of Love" (Bon Jovi; 4:14)
3. "Only Lonely" (Bon Jovi, David Bryan; 5:02)
4. "King of the Mountain" (Bon Jovi, Richie Sambora; 3:54)
5. "Silent Night" (Bon Jovi; 5:07)
Side two
6. "Tokyo Road" (Bon Jovi, Sambora; 5:41)
7. "The Hardest Part Is the Night" (Bon Jovi, Bryan, Sambora; 4:25)
8. "Always Run to You" (Bon Jovi, Sambora; 5:00)
9. "(I Don't Wanna Fall) to the Fire" (Bon Jovi, Bryan, Sambora; 4:27)
10. "Secret Dreams" (Bon Jovi, Sambora, Tico Torres, Bill Grabowski; 4:56)

A couple of ominous signs surrounded the making of the album. Speaking to Sylvie Simmons of *Request Magazine* in 1996, Jon recalled: "I remember going through some legal hassles with a production company that claimed we had a deal with them and wanted a piece of the band because now all of a sudden we were touting our success. And we literally had to carry the tapes with us to and from the studio for fear of somebody stealing them."

Partway through recording, Bon Jovi's rehearsal studio in Perth Amboy, New Jersey, had been broken into and much of their gear stolen. Doc McGhee put up a $2,500 reward for information leading to the return of the instruments and gear. Derek Shulman recalls that nothing was ever recovered.

After the album's release, Bon Jovi hit the road again. The first stop on the band's tour was Japan. They went on to play the World Music Festival with Deep Purple in Dallas in August followed by two dates at the Monsters of Rock Festival at Castle Donington in the United Kingdom. They came back to play a Cotton Bowl festival in Dallas with Scorpions, Ted Nugent, and ZZ Top, then the first Farm Aid in Austin, Texas, on September 22 with a diverse roster including John Denver, Huey Lewis, X, and Van Halen. During the year, Jon was briefly involved with actress Diane Lane, but by year's end he had returned to his hometown to win back Dorothea and reignite their relationship, which was to become a cornerstone in his life.

Regular touring resumed in mid-October when they joined Ratt's extensive American trek, opening for them through the end of the year. "I saw one of those shows, and they were great," says Joe Franco, veteran rock drummer and owner of Beatstreet Productions. (He had briefly filled in for Tico after he left Frankie and the Knockouts.) "Sambora was great. They were like fucking rock stars. They had the arena thing down."

> ❝ YOU KNOW WHAT'S FUNNY IS THE ALBUM [*7800° FAHRENHEIT*] SOLD TWICE AS MANY COPIES [AS THE FIRST], BUT IT IS MY LEAST FAVORITE ALBUM IN RETROSPECT. IT WAS A VERY . . . NOT PAINFUL TIME, BUT YOU KNOW [HOW] YOU HAVE YOUR WHOLE LIFE TO WRITE YOUR FIRST ALBUM? YOU HAVE SIX WEEKS TO WRITE THE SECOND ONE. ❞
>
> **Jon Bon Jovi** to Sylvie Simmons of *Request* magazine, 1996

FROM JERSEY TO JAPAN

ABOVE LEFT: A poster for the 1986 Castle Donington lineup, which featured an eclectic mix: Southern blues band ZZ Top, prog rockers Marillion, and hard rockers Bon Jovi and Ratt.

ABOVE RIGHT: PolyGram's Barry Fisch presents Jon with a gold record certifying shipments of 500,000 copies of *7800° Fahrenheit*. Although more successful than their debut, expectations had been much higher for the record.

Along the way the members of Bon Jovi did press with MTV and any radio, video, and print outlets that could give them exposure. Despite nonstop touring and regular promotion, the album (unlike its title) was not catching fire the way they had hoped. (Funnily enough, *7800° Fahrenheit* referred to the fictitious, and subsequently erroneously reported, melting point of rock. The real temperature is closer to 2300°F.)

"There was a lot of concern around the time of *7800°* because it was expected to be the record that was going to really blow it up, and when it didn't there was a lot of panic," recalls radio, television, and music industry veteran Eddie Trunk in our interview. "I remember working in a record store, and the hype and the push for *7800°* to be the breaking record was pretty sizable. When it didn't happen there was concern that maybe this band wasn't going to go the distance like everybody thought. Here in New Jersey it was still a big deal, and the records were still getting played. When they shot those videos on the boardwalk there was a lot of people that went to see them. But nationally it didn't catch. I have a 12-inch radio promo for 'Silent Night' and the picture on the cover is Jon and it says, 'The best kept secret in radio,' because they just couldn't get it over nationally."

The band needed a creative shot in the arm, especially as they were in the midst of what would eventually become a six-year grind of making an album and touring, then back to the studio again.

The stakes had been raised. Although Bon Jovi had toured hard and sales were up over their debut (750,000 versus 350,000), *7800° Fahrenheit* was not destined to be the release that broke the band to a massive audience. When they set about crafting their third album, it was make or break time. And they would answer that challenge with their biggest statement ever.

VIDEO EVOLUTION

THE CLIPS THAT HELPED MAKE BON JOVI FAMOUS AND THOSE WHICH STARTED THEIR CAREER WERE STRIKINGLY DIFFERENT.

Prior to Wayne Isham's iconic performance clips, conceptual videos by other directors were shot to coincide with single releases. The aforementioned "Runaway" kickstarted Bon Jovi's video profile, and while its dramatic scenes left a lot to be desired, it was the band's presence that made it memorable.

The follow-up clip for "She Don't Know Me" featured denim-clad Jon pining for a woman he loved (future *Terminator* movie star Linda Hamilton) but who secretly watched and followed him in his torment. Meanwhile another woman longed for him. The video played on Jon's sex appeal, and his tight jeans and nicely coiffed hair were designed to please female fans. During various press interviews in the mid-1980s, Jon voiced his distaste for many of their early videos.

For the first video from their sophomore album, "Only Lonely," they brought director Jack Cole on board. Cole had worked with Styx frontman Dennis DeYoung on "Desert Moon" and Journey singer Steve Perry on "Oh Sherrie," and he was one of the first directors to regularly inject dialogue into music videos.

While visiting MTV's *Heavy Metal Mania* in 1985, Jon told host Dee Snider that he had written a storyline relatable to the personal life of the director, who suggested that they film a mini-movie. The frontman approved, but it ultimately turned out to be something Jon would not go and see—the cryptic storyline involving a struggling band, the singer's girlfriend whose parents disapprove of their relationship, a corrupt band manager, and thugs seeking payback for being ratted out. It mirrored many angst-ridden rebel teen films of the era and initially fooled some people into thinking that there was a real movie forthcoming. Young fans on YouTube today have thought the same thing at first glance.

When their next video for the anthemic opening track "In and Out of Love" was created—and it was the best of the bunch—it focused on a band performance on a Jersey boardwalk intercut with them mingling with fans, flirting with hot babes, and hiding from crazed groupies, specifically in two scenes that recalled the Beatles' film *A Hard Day's Night*. The bookends to the clip were Bon Jovi's arrival from London and departure to Japan, emphasizing their growing global appeal.

For the third and final clip from *7800° Fahrenheit*, the ballad "Silent Night" received an innovative treatment from director Marcelo Epstein. A quarreling couple were isolated in a room, where projected upon three walls was footage of their happier past intercut with a band performance. More typical of their downbeat early period, this would be the last video to have a serious storyline for a while. Starting with their next album, director Wayne Isham would change the game. The time for tales had passed. It was time to rock the house.

ABOVE: Bon Jovi filming their first video "Runaway" at Silvercup Studios in Queens, New York, in December 1983.

❝ [THE EARLY VIDEOS] WERE CHEESY AS HELL. THEY WERE AWFUL. 'RUNAWAY'... EVEN THEN WHILE IT WAS HAPPENING, WE COULD TELL IT WOULD TURN OUT AS CHEESY AS IT DID. WE ALL LOOKED AT IT THINKING, 'HOLY SHIT, WHY DID WE DO THAT?' I DON'T REMEMBER THE OTHER [EARLY] VIDEOS. OBVIOUSLY THE WAYNE ISHAM ONES HAD BIGGER BUDGETS AND WERE MUCH BETTER, AND WAYNE WAS A GREAT DIRECTOR. FOR THE MOST PART, PEOPLE JUST REMEMBER THE *SLIPPERY* ONES, WHICH ARE PRETTY SPECTACULAR. ❞

Derek Shulman, April 2016

IV

WILD IN THE STREETS

1986—1987

THE STAGE WAS SET. THEY WERE RIDING THE CUSP OF FAME. BUT COULD THEY BREAK THROUGH TO SUPERSTARDOM?

Continuing what would ultimately become a punishing six-year album-tour-album-tour cycle, the musical gang in Bon Jovi did not take too much time off after closing the Ratt tour with a New Year's gig at the Sports Arena in San Diego. During the first half of 1986, they plunged into the writing and recording of their biggest and most important album ever—*Slippery When Wet*.

A major change was needed. The band needed a bigger, bolder sound. Derek Shulman suggested Bruce Fairbairn, who had produced Loverboy, Krokus, and Blue Öyster Cult. Jon liked the idea, but first he and Richie needed to get down to the business of writing songs together, banging out ideas with acoustic guitars and a tape recorder, working in Richie's parents' basement. One of the first compositions completed was "Wanted Dead or Alive," an atmospheric, beguiling ballad that equated their lives on the road with Wild West outlaws moving from town to town. Inspired by Bob Seger's "Turn the Page," the tune would later be referred to by Jon as the group's "national anthem." Working off a lyrical idea that Jon previously had, he and Richie allegedly wrote it in about three hours.

Beyond penning that anthem, the songwriting duo realized that they needed a third party to come in and help them in their writing endeavors. They had explored the tried and true themes of love, heartbreak, and life on the road—which, to be fair, encapsulated their lives at that point—but a fresh voice could help them take their work to the next level. They also contemplated selling songs to other artists.

Shulman says that he brought songwriter Desmond Child into the picture after a referral from KISS bassist Gene Simmons. Child was the former singer and member of the group Rouge, which had a short-lived, two-album career in the late 1970s and recorded the Top 50 hit "Our Love Is Insane." He had scored a hit with KISS ("I Was Made For Loving You") and then pumped out some harder rocking tunes for that band's subsequent *Animalize* and *Asylum* albums, which strongly boosted both of their careers.

Combining forces with these Jersey boys would prove to be a brilliant move. Child went to an initial meeting with Jon and Richie at the latter's parents' very modest home in Woodbridge, New Jersey, which was located near a marsh and an oil refinery and was a contrast to Jon's

PAGE 54: A leather-clad Jon Bon Jovi trying to rev up a Judas Priest audience during the band's opening slot for the heavy metal legends on July 23, 1986, in Montreal, Canada.

ABOVE: The members of Bon Jovi manning the decks with the late producer Bruce Fairbairn (front row, far right) at Little Mountain Studios in Vancouver, during spring 1986.

parents' more middle-class surburban home. Rather spontaneously "You Give Love a Bad Name" was born from that session, and it was the first of many hits that they would crank out together. Their chemistry was instant and tangible. They penned more songs, two of which made the album: "Without Love" and "Livin' on a Prayer." Whereas earlier Bon Jovi recordings had a more melancholic flavor, the new compositions were far more upbeat in tone.

Interestingly enough, "Bad Name," about knowingly being attracted to a toxic lover, was actually a reworking of a disco-ish song that Child had written for Bonnie Tyler a few months earlier called "If You Were a Woman (and I Was a Man)" which had barely charted in America at that time, eventually peaking at Number 77. Speaking to Paul Child of the *Welsh Show* in the United Kingdom in April 2013, Desmond Child explained, "That song actually became a big hit in France, but it really wasn't the hit that I wanted it to be because when I wrote it I said, 'This is going to be the biggest song of all time.'"

When he had the opportunity to collaborate with Jon and Richie, Desmond decided to rework the tune. The a cappella opening, the strutting verses, and the vocal melody and harmonies in the chorus were nearly identical. "I was sore at the [other] record company for not pushing that [original] song," Child recalled on the Welsh Show, "so I said, 'I'm going to prove that that song's a hit." So we did." The difference, of course, is that Bon Jovi rocked it up. In a June 2015 podcast with Decibel Geek, Child recalled that Jon and Richie probably weren't aware that he was incorporating elements from the previous tune. Shulman tells me that the Tyler song was not on PolyGram's radar. (Further, Jon took the first lyrical phrase, "Shot Through the Heart," from a song title on his band's debut album.) Reborn as "You Give Love a Bad Name," this new creation would soon turn into one of Bon Jovi's signature rockers.

As became the norm for future Bon Jovi releases, Jon and Richie (and their respective collaborators) produced way more songs than they needed. In this case, thirty-five in total, of which twenty to twenty-two were reportedly demoed. In keeping with their desire to please their fans, the two songwriters have claimed they tested out the demos they recorded in New Jersey to kids at a local pizza parlor (now known as the "Pizza Parlor Jury"). But the real test would come when the songs were put to tape.

❝ I SAT DOWN AND LISTENED TO *SLIPPERY* AND WAS LIKE, 'WHAT THE FUCK?' I DIDN'T HEAR THE DESMOND DEMOS. JON SAID, 'WHAT DO YOU THINK?' I SAID, 'DUDE, THIS IS IT.' HE SAID, 'THE RECORD COMPANY THINKS WE CAN PROBABLY GO GOLD WITH THIS.' I SAID, 'I'LL GUARANTEE YOU THIS IS GOING TO BE PLATINUM.' I FORGET WHAT WE BET ON, BUT HE STILL OWES ME THAT BET. IT WAS JUST THE PERFECT STORM, AND WITHOUT DESMOND THAT WOULDN'T HAVE HAPPENED. ❞

Jack Ponti, January 2016

58   In April 1986, Bon Jovi departed for Little Mountain Studios in Vancouver. They rented a condo and spent six weeks rehearsing and recording with producer Bruce Fairbairn and engineer Bob Rock, who had worked with Fairbairn before and would later become famous for producing Mötley Crüe and Metallica. While this production team would give Bon Jovi the sonic boom they needed, Jon was not convinced about Fairbairn initially when they met with him in Jersey.

"I listened to the songs for a few days, just to see what they had," Fairbairn told Steve Newton (earofnewt.com) of the Vancouver newspaper, the *Georgia Straight*, on November 12, 1998. "Then Jon and I went for a ride, and he said, 'Bruce, you're not doin' it.' And I go, 'Oh? Whaddya mean?' And he says, 'Well, you're not sayin' much; you're not comin' to the party.' And I went, 'Well, that's not my style, Jon; I want to try and find out what's at the party before I try and move the venue.'" Jack Ponti also recalls Jon expressing his lack of enthusiasm while in Jersey.

Soon enough the party was happening in Vancouver—Jon's attitude shifted positively after that, as Jack confirms—and not just in the studio. Fairbairn was known for being a methodical taskmaster, and he made the band bring their A-game. At night, the boys hit the streets of Vancouver to enjoy the benefits of booze, cards, and strippers. Expo86, a World's Fair, was also taking place, instilling extra energy into the city. At that point, few of the band members were really attached, so they could indulge in the wild life, and that unbridled hedonism oozed into the grooves of the album. Songs like "Let It Rock," "Raise Your Hands," and "Wild in the Streets" were performed with gusto and set the scene for a rowdy night out on the town.

"They came in like a gang from New Jersey to do pre-production," Bob Rock recalled to *Music Radar*'s Joe Bosso on March 13, 2013. "But they had fun, too: they invaded all the strip joints and completely obliterated the city. We recorded all of the basics in the studio live off the floor. Everything was done very quickly. When Bruce and I finished it, we thought the song that could be a hit was 'Livin' on a Prayer.' I remember having a conversation with him at the board, and he said, 'Well, I hope the record goes gold so we can get some more work.'

ABOVE: British ad from 1987 promoting the "Livin' on a Prayer" single and tour dates in the United Kingdom.

OPPOSITE: Promotional button, showing the patriotic Jon with full mane flowing.

SLIPPERY WHEN WET ALBUM

Release dates: August 18, 1986 (US); September 8, 1986 (UK)
Recording studio: Little Mountain Sound Studios, Vancouver, BC
Producer: Bruce Fairbairn
Engineer: Bob Rock
Singles: "You Give Love a Bad Name," "Livin' on a Prayer,"
"Wanted Dead or Alive," "Never Say Goodbye"
Top chart position: 1 (US, *Billboard*); 1 (UK)

Side one
1. "Let It Rock" (Jon Bon Jovi, Richie Sambora; 5:27)
2. "You Give Love a Bad Name" (Bon Jovi, Sambora,
   Desmond Child; 3:42)
3. "Livin' on a Prayer" (Bon Jovi, Sambora, Child; 4:09)
4. "Social Disease" (Bon Jovi, Sambora; 4:18)
5. "Wanted Dead or Alive" (Bon Jovi, Sambora; 5:08)

Side two
6. "Raise Your Hands" (Bon Jovi, Sambora; 4:16)
7. "Without Love" (Bon Jovi, Sambora, Child; 3:30)
8. "I'd Die for You" (Bon Jovi, Sambora, Child; 4:30)
9. "Never Say Goodbye" (Bon Jovi, Sambora; 4:48)
10. "Wild in the Streets" (Bon Jovi; 3:54)

That's as high as we were aiming. The record was one of those magical things where everything works. The engineering and mixing that I did, everything Bruce did, the way the band wrote with Desmond Child—it all came together."

"It was an incredible atmosphere and an incredible situation," Derek Shulman recalls of the sessions. "It could not have been better because you had Bob Rock, who's an incredible engineer, and Bruce Fairbairn, who was a spectacular producer. Very down to earth, but kept the clock ticking and really made it the way it was. It was a lot of fun after and before the sessions, but during the sessions it was very professional."

If one listens to the various *Slippery* demos that have surfaced on YouTube, it is easy to hear how Fairbairn and Rock helped imbue the tunes with the sonic sheen they needed to sparkle on radio. The songs were there, but Fairbairn gave them space and thickened the guitars and vocal harmonies. "You Give Love a Bad Name" received boisterous vocal harmonies and guitar hooks absent from the demo. The amped-up guitars of "Raise Your Hands" dominated over the poppy keyboards of the original version.

"Livin' on a Prayer" got the biggest facelift. The guitar line in the verse changed, Sambora brought in the famous talk-box riff, the bass work had more groove, and rousing vocal harmonies were injected. In an interview with Stacy McCloud on WZTV Fox 17 in March 2013, Desmond Child said that the "Tommy and Gina" of the lyrical story were inspired by his personal experiences with an old girlfriend named Maria Vidal during their years of struggle. Originally, the characters were called Johnny and Gina. Desmond's birth name was John Charles Barrett, and Maria's nickname as a singing waitress was Gina. "Jon said, 'I can't sing Johnny, my name's Johnny . . . then it sounds like it's about me'," Child recalled on WZTV. So, the name was changed to Tommy, which had a similar alliterative quality.

The song became an instant classic. Funnily enough, Jon did not hear the potential at first. "The fact is, Jon didn't want to record it," Child told WZTV. "So Richie and I literally had to get on our hands and knees and beg him to." Jon also contemplated giving "You Give Love a Bad Name" to Loverboy. Instead, they got the minor hit "Notorious."

MODEL CONTROVERSY

CREATING THE FAMOUS COVER FOR *SLIPPERY WHEN WET* TURNED OUT TO BE A MORE DIFFICULT TASK THAN INITIALLY THOUGHT.

Given the fact that Jon had started developing a cowboy fetish and had co-written the now iconic "Wanted Dead or Alive" (the original album title) with Richie for the album, the idea of doing a photo shoot with the band members done up as outlaws seemed like a no-brainer. Apparently neither their label nor manager Doc McGhee thought the concept clicked, at least not for the album; however, famed rock photographer Mark Weiss's western-themed shoot would later be used for the "Wanted" single.

Something sexier was devised for the album, and Mark set about finding the right model for a racy picture to grace *Slippery*'s cover. The result was an image of a busty woman's chest in a tight T-shirt sporting the album title with water being splashed on her. Given that it was the Decade of Decadence, one might have thought the cover would have been considered a good selling point. It was not, especially with large retail chains potentially refusing to stock something that salacious.

The album's title was inspired by some soaped-up nude dancers that had beguiled Doc and the band in Vancouver. The cover shot reflected that idea. "The album art was pulled as the album was about to ship to retail," reveals Shulman, who had been on the road with the band and had not yet seen the risqué imagery. "The original idea was more the art department coming up with something that was deemed to be titillating and tantalizing. When the cover art was finally revealed Doc McGhee and myself thought it looked like an ad for [what would today be] a porn site. The resulting about-face happened in probably twenty-four hours."

Derek, Doc, and Jon met at the PolyGram offices while the original albums were being pressed. "I ordered that the album stopped pressing with the original art," says Shulman. "It was finally Jon who grabbed a garbage bag and sprayed it with water and wrote 'Slippery When Wet' on it. All Mark Weiss had to do was photograph this image on the table, which took all of two minutes. Obviously it worked even though the music would have been enough with a brown paper bag. I believe that we were too late to pull the original cover art from the Japanese release. This is why the 'artwork' is still known to exist." (The racy image was used for 1986 Japanese concert tour programs.)

It is rumored that a quarter of a million copies were destroyed, but Doc McGhee has said about 40,000 were pressed initially. "They only destroyed the artwork," clarifies Barry Fisch, formerly of PolyGram. "They pressed the vinyl. I don't think they destroyed that. If a record was retailing for $7.98, $8.98, or $9.98, I think the manufacturing cost as a whole was about two bucks [per unit]. It cost them some money, but if it cost them a couple hundred thousand dollars to destroy the artwork that was chump change."

Brand new copies of those rarely seen Japanese albums have been listed recently on eBay for at least $199.99.

OPPOSITE: The banned *Slippery When Wet* cover that still managed to get released in Japan. While it would have been suitable for many Sunset Strip bands of the that era, it was deemed too raunchy for Bon Jovi.

BON JOVI

❝ WE KNEW THE MUSIC WAS ABSOLUTELY THE VERY BEST
ROCK ALBUM EVER MADE AT THE TIME, AND TO HAVE THIS
ALBUM ART 'SPOILING' WHAT WAS MAGICAL IN THE GROOVES
WOULD HAVE BEEN A DISASTER. ❞

Derek Shulman, February 2016

The big sound of the album would also prove to be influential on other late 1980s hard rock releases. "Those big floor-tom hits became such a thing," recalls drummer Joe Franco when we speak. "Drum production became so huge back in that era, so when those big floor-tom hits came down on the backbeat it became an arena rock staple. I can't tell you how many times [they] were used after that. You've heard them a zillion times."

Upon its August 1986 release, *Slippery When Wet* already started making waves. The first single, "You Give Love a Bad Name," had hit the airwaves and stores a month earlier, and momentum was slowly building. While many songs today quickly explode because of the spontaneous exposure across online outlets, radio and MTV were the mainstays of public awareness back in the eighties. The band set off to promote the album with a short Canadian tour opening for metal icons Judas Priest in July before heading to Japan.

Judas Priest frontman Rob Halford recollects that Bon Jovi did not have an easy go of things when faced with rabid Priest fans, even if it was during Priest's more commercial *Turbo* phase. But they gave it their all. "Literally every night they faced some kind of challenging situation," says Halford. And he admired their spirit. "They must've known before they walked out onstage at a Priest show that they had to work their asses off there. They did their best to bring over some Priest fans, and I'm sure they did."

Following their subsequent Japanese trek, Bon Jovi opened for .38 Special in the States, then undertook a headlining European jaunt with support act Queensrÿche. "They hit some tours at the right time," observes photographer Eddie Malluk. "They were opening for Ratt when Ratt exploded, and they beat out Ratt [live]. They opened for .38 Special when they put out the *Slippery* album, and they were drawing more people than .38 Special on that tour."

While they were overseas, "Bad Name" hit Number 1 the week of November 29 after twenty-four weeks on the chart. The tide had turned. Bon Jovi had truly arrived. And the topsy-turvy rollercoaster ride was just beginning. Starting in mid-December, the band

TOP: Jon, Tico, and Alec taking their bow after an opening slot for Judas Priest in Montreal, July 23, 1986. Their camaraderie shines through in this photo.

BOTTOM: A ticket from Bon Jovi's opening show for .38 Special at the Meadowlands in New Jersey on September 12, 1986.

undertook a massive, eight-month headlining tour of America, with rising stars Cinderella, whom Jon had helped secure a deal for at the same label as Bon Jovi, opening most of the dates.

In February, after spending twenty-one weeks on the charts, the second *Slippery* single, "Livin' on a Prayer," hit Number 1, and the band became a household name through constant radio and MTV exposure. Their success also had a dramatic effect on the industry. While the first wave of hair bands had already happened, Bon Jovi opened the door, for better or worse, for an even bigger wave of clones, this time many of them emulating the Jersey rockers.

"As much as the hair bands were getting bigger, you never really heard them on radio," observes veteran rock journalist Gail Flug in our interview. "All of the hair metal bands in the early '80s were broken by MTV. Bon Jovi was the one that broke the doors down and made it more mainstream and more accessible, because then rock radio/AOR stations were starting to play 'Rock Me' and 'Once Bitten, Twice Shy' by Great White. Then 'Still of the Night' by Whitesnake. I think the reason that Whitesnake changed their image was because they needed to look good and appeal to a Bon Jovi crowd."

Bon Jovi had one more hit to come from *Slippery*. The band's rock cowboy song "Wanted Dead or Alive" peaked at Number 7 in June, making them the first hard rock group to have three Top 10 singles on the same album. Although the last single and video "Never Say Goodbye" did not chart, it did not matter. Album sales skyrocketed and *Slippery When Wet* became the biggest selling release of 1987, ultimately racking up over eight million units in total, with half of them sold that year. At one point during its original run, *Slippery* was selling a million copies a month. By 1995 it had sold another four million units, making it one of the RIAA's Top 100 releases of all time.

The year of 1987 was filled with achievements. Jon and Richie co-penned tunes that went on to be recorded by Cher and Loverboy. The band headlined the Monsters of Rock festival in Germany in August, with heavy metal acts like Metallica, Dio, and Anthrax on the bill.

▟▟ I REMEMBER WHEN JON AND RICHIE PLAYED ME 'WANTED DEAD OR ALIVE.' THEY SAID, 'WHAT DO YOU THINK?' I SAID, 'I THINK IT'S A GREAT SONG, BUT YOU'RE SAYING I'M A COWBOY. SHOULDN'T IT BE *LIKE* A COWBOY? BECAUSE YOU'RE NOT COWBOYS.' THEY LOOKED AT ME AND BLINKED A COUPLE OF TIMES AND SAID, 'WE'LL PLAY YOU THE NEXT TUNE.' I LEARNED SO MUCH FROM THEM AT THAT MOMENT. I'M A REALIST. BUT JON KNEW WHO HIS AUDIENCE WAS. HE SAID, 'LET'S FACE IT, MAN, OUR AUDIENCE IS ELEVEN- TO SIXTEEN-YEAR-OLD GIRLS, SO HOW FAR ARE WE GOING TO GO AWAY FROM THAT RIGHT NOW? WE'RE GONNA LOSE 'EM. WE'RE IN THIS MOMENT, WE HAVE TO TAKE THEM ON THE JOURNEY AND LET THEM GROW UP WITH US.' HE WAS VERY, VERY WISE WITH THAT BECAUSE THEY SAID *I'M* A COWBOY. THEY WENT ALL THE WAY, AND THAT WAS THE THING I LEARNED THAT DAY. WHEN YOU'RE DOING IT, YOU GO ALL THE WAY. ▙▙

Bruce Stephen Foster, Grammy-nominated singer-songwriter, February 2016

BON JOVI

WANTED
DEAD OR
ALIVE

◆

THE CRIME

7" with FREE METAL STICKERS
12" SILVER VINYL with 2 EXTRA LIVE TRACKS

◆

REWARD

TOTAL LISTENING PLEASURE
OUT NOW

◆

7" JOVS 1 12" JOVR 112

Further accolades included Favorite Pop/Rock Band at the American Music Awards and Favorite Rock Group at the People's Choice Awards.

At the MTV Music Video Awards, they won Best Stage Performance for "Livin' on a Prayer" and played it live that night. Jon graced the cover of the five-hundredth issue of *Rolling Stone*, which had dissed their latest album the year before, likening it to third-rate hard rock. But they acknowledged the band's established stardom with the slightly snarky cover story "The Kids Are Alright."

On the flip side of the sold-out shows and fan adulation, Jon began struggling with his voice. The band's jump from being openers with a shorter set to headliners required them to deliver more energy for longer periods of time every night. Fatigue was setting in, but the band kept charging ahead.

Still, Bon Jovi were on top of the world then. "*Slippery When Wet* was the pinnacle," confirms Flug. "When they played in New York, they played three nights at the Garden, two nights at the Meadowlands, and two nights at Nassau Coliseum, which is unheard of. They can't do that now, and they probably can never do that again."

"The first night there [at the Garden] it was like seeing the Beatles," says Malluk. "It was insane. You couldn't hear yourself think. You got goose pimples. When they came out for the first two or three songs it was a spectacle. It was incredible. I've seen I don't how many thousands of shows, and it's rare where you see something special like that."

They had hit the top. But was it all downhill from there? Far from it. Great things were yet to come.

PAGE 65: Jersey boys dressed as outlaw cowboys for the "Wanted Dead or Alive" single. This was the original cover concept for the *Slippery When Wet* album, which initially was intended to be titled after this western-themed single.

ABOVE AND OPPOSITE: Jon and Richie displaying their patriotism onstage at a show in Illinois, in early March 1987. They have always been proud of being an American band.

THE ISHAM FACTOR

THE VIDEO CLIPS FOR THE FIRST TWO BON JOVI ALBUMS, WHILE OCCASIONALLY SELLING THE BAND THANKS TO THEIR ENERGETIC PERFORMANCES, FAILED TO SEDUCE A LARGER FANBASE IN A WAY THAT WOULD LEAD TO PLATINUM SUCCESS.

Part of that may have been the songs, but MTV had ushered in an era of high style, and Bon Jovi, becoming more robustly colorful than ever during the *Slippery When Wet* period, needed to capitalize on their fashion sense as well as the poster boy looks of Jon and Richie.

For the first video on *Slippery When Wet*, Bon Jovi recruited innovative music video director Wayne Isham, whose credits included Mötley Crüe, Dokken, and Judas Priest. Rather than attempt another conceptual clip, Isham focused on what had helped fuel Bon Jovi's rise up the ranks: their spirited, all-or-nothing shows. He knew how to coax great performances out of anyone he filmed. Before Wayne, the band hated making videos. Through him, they embraced the medium.

The first clip from *Slippery*, the anthemic "You Give Love a Bad Name," zeroed in on their energy and onstage camaraderie. Isham and his team rented out an abandoned boxing arena for an afternoon, painted the band's name on the stage, and enticed Bon Jovi fans down with the prospect of watching the quintet film and getting some between-take performances. The trick worked and the resultant video, complete with a massive rig shooting light down on the band like a flying saucer, transformed them into arena rock gods.

That approach continued with "Livin' on a Prayer," except this time the clip started with black-and-white rehearsal footage of the band in the same empty venue (the two clips were shot back to back) before it exploded into full color and full audience intensity. The video featured Jon flying over the audience in a harness, which became a required staple of each concert as fans expected that after seeing it onscreen. (The stunt also inspired Jon's Superman tattoo on his left bicep.) Echoing the outlaw sentiments of its lyrics, the black-and-white "Wanted Dead or Alive" clip, this time actually shot on tour, showed the weary band giving their all in performances to ecstatic crowds then looking drained by the end. It was meant to invoke sympathy for the hardworking hard rockers, and it succeeded. The lesser seen "Never Say Goodbye" and "Wild in the Streets" combined raw concert footage with childhood band member photos (for the former) and backstage and street shenanigans with hot girls (in the latter).

Isham made five videos for *Slippery*, and he returned for six more on the follow-up album *New Jersey*, the first being "Bad Medicine," which flipped the script by giving audience members video cameras to shoot the band from their various perspectives. The resultant low-fi assemblage predated the grainy footage that became requisite for many nineties videos. Getting back to professional cinematography, "I'll Be There for You," and "Lay Your Hands on Me" followed the same live template as its predecessors. "Blood on Blood" was actually a bonafide live per-formance, while "Born to Be My Baby" replicated them recording in a studio. For "Living in Sin," Wayne dived into a conceptual piece, intercutting band performance footage with a story about a young couple in love and sexually engaged, with the girl's disapproving parents seeking to sever their ties. It was a distinctly eighties theme that was well executed.

Since the 1980s, Wayne has directed numerous clips for the band, and for Jon and Richie in their solo careers. He has been an indelible influence on the music video genre and on Bon Jovi's career. "A part of what our videos were, and I think that's why Wayne is relevant and why we're still around, is because it's almost a documentary," Sambora told TV program, *Video Killed the Radio Star* in 2010. "[You saw] what was happening to our lives as it was happening."

OPPOSITE: Music video director Wayne Isham with his Lifetime Achievement Award at the sixteenth Annual Music Video Production Association Awards on May 16, 2007. Beyond his work for Bon Jovi, among his many famous videos are Mötley Crüe's "Dr. Feelgood," Metallica's "Enter Sandman," and Ricky Martin's "Livin' la Vida Loca."

❝ I LOVE METAL AND ROCK MUSIC, AND I APPRECIATE A GREAT SHOW. SO WHEN THE OPPORTUNITY CAME UP FOR BON JOVI, I SAID, 'I KNOW WHAT TO DO. WE'RE GOING TO DO A GREAT MOCK LIVE SHOW FOR JON AND REALLY SHOW HIS CHARACTER, HIS FORTE.' ❞

Wayne Isham, *Video Killed the Radio Star*, 2010

V

MAXIMUM OVERDRIVE

1988—1990

AFTER THE WEARYING WORLDWIDE TREK OF 1986–1987 SUPPORTING *SLIPPERY WHEN WET*, ONE MIGHT THINK THAT A VACATION WAS IN ORDER. AND FOR NOVEMBER AT LEAST, THE MEMBERS OF BON JOVI GOT SOME TIME OFF. BUT PERENNIAL WORKHORSE JON AND HIS SONGWRITING PARTNER RICHIE WERE SOON JUMPING BACK INTO MAKING DEMOS FOR THEIR FOURTH ALBUM. THE THEMES THIS TIME NATURALLY INCLUDED LOVE AND LUST, BUT LOYALTY AND FRIENDSHIP WERE STRONG THREADS THAT RAN THROUGH THE COLLECTION.

Jon Bon Jovi recalled to *Classic Rock* magazine in 2003 that as the initial sessions began, he and Richie struggled to come up with that big song that would put them over the top. Pleased with the ecstatic response to their previous collaborative efforts, they reteamed with Desmond Child and conjured many fresh tunes including "Bad Medicine," "Born to Be My Baby," "Blood on Blood," "Wild Is the Wind" (also co-authored with perennial hitmaker Diane Warren), "Let's Make It Baby," "Love Is War," "Does Anybody Really Fall in Love Anymore?," and "Diamond Ring." The first four made the album. The last track appeared on *These Days* in 1995, "Love Is War" became a B-side, and ". . . Fall in Love . . ." was later recorded by Cher and Kane Roberts separately. Jon and Richie also collaborated with Holly Knight on "Stick to Your Guns."

Between May and July, Bon Jovi were back up in Vancouver banging out a new album with the titanic team of Fairbairn and Rock. The group's musical palette had now expanded thanks to increased proficiency on their instruments and their latest collaborations. There was more bluesiness to some of the new tunes, notably "Homebound Train," the acoustic "Ride Cowboy Ride" (a mono intro to "Stick to Your Guns"), and the album closer "Love for Sale," a bluesy acoustic jam that offered a nice contrast to the album's general bombast. (That latter song was, unlike the rest of the album, recorded in New Jersey.) Richie played a pastoral Spanish guitar intro to the raucous "Wild Is the Wind." The vocal harmonies on the choruses of "Lay Your Hands on Me" were enriched by the gospel-like inflections of the

PAGE 70: A euphoric Richie Sambora gives his all on the New Jersey Syndicate tour in 1989.

OPPOSITE: An American magazine ad for *New Jersey*. Note how Jon is separated from the rest of the band, further identifying him as the ringleader.

73

❞ WE BROUGHT IN FIFTY KIDS TO THE STUDIO, AND WE PLAYED THEM EVERYTHING. IT WAS SURPRISINGLY HELPFUL BECAUSE AGAIN A COUPLE OF SONGS WOULDN'T HAVE MADE IT, AND WHAT SURPRISED ME IS THE ORDER THEY PICKED THEM IN. BUT THE GREATEST THING WE'VE DONE THAT I'M READING IN MAGAZINES NOW, WHICH IS GREAT, IS THAT OTHER BANDS ARE DOING WHAT WE DID. IT ONLY MAKES SENSE TO GO TO THE KIDS. THEY'RE THE PEOPLE THAT BUY IT. IT WAS GREAT BECAUSE WE LOSE TOUCH WITH THE STUFF. WE WRITE IT, SO YOU DON'T KNOW ANYMORE. ❞

Jon Bon Jovi, *New Jersey* press conference, August 18, 1988

Sweet Thing Vocal Association, which included singer Sue Leonard, who has since worked with k.d. lang.

"Homebound Train" offered David Bryan that rare chance to show off his chops, given that Bon Jovi is more of a guitar-centric band. Before Richie ripped into his big solo, David battled Jon in a three-part trade-off of the singer's wailing harmonica against the keyboardist's hot organ licks. While the prelude to the previous album allowed David to create an intense, Jon Lord-like intro, on "Homebound Train" he let loose.

The resultant album maintained the vibe of its predecessor while offering some new ideas. But when they initially arrived in Vancouver with thirty new songs, Jon and Richie had a lot to wade through, and they felt the pressure of following up one of the biggest rock albums ever.

Listening to the demo outtakes now, it is apparent that Jon and Richie struggled somewhat to escape the vibe of *Slippery*. The "na-na-na" chant from "Born to Be My Baby" also surfaced on "Judgement Day" and "Let's Make It Baby." "Backdoor to Heaven" had a familiar power-ballad stamp. And while catchy, "Love Is War" rather mimicked the chorus of "You Give Love a Bad Name."

Like the Pizza Parlor Jury in Jersey with *Slippery When Wet*, Bon Jovi brought in some Vancouver locals for a taste test of the ultimately titled *New Jersey*.

When asked at the August 18th press conference for the album release about the concept of New Jersey as an attitude and how it was put into the record, Tico replied, "The attitude's from the heart. It's a New Jersey vibe. It's where we came from, that's where we'll probably die, but we want to share it with the world."

Bon Jovi originally wanted to release *New Jersey* as a double album in a two-for-one deal for fans, but Mercury was against the idea. Judas Priest had tried the same thing with *Turbo* in 1986, and Columbia/CBS also vetoed their plan. Thus the Jersey boys distilled their efforts down to twelve tracks. Different album titles had allegedly been toyed with, including *Sons of Beaches* and the ridiculous *Sixty-Eight and I'll Owe You One*, but it seemed fitting to title the effort after their home state since their Jersey pride was always strong.

The band had occasionally ridden the edge of salaciousness without crossing the line. Part of that was just circumstance, part of it was wiser judgment prevailing. Nixing the sexy

OPPOSITE: The boys in the band play a game of musical chairs to fool unsuspecting shutterbugs and journalists at a *New Jersey* press conference in August 1, 1988. Left to right: Tico Torres, David Bryan, Jon Bon Jovi, Richie Sambora, and Alec John Such.

ALEC JOHN SUCH   JON BON JOVI   RICHIE SAMBORA   TICO TORRES   DAVID BRYAN

NEW JERSEY ALBUM

Release date: September 19, 1988
Recording studio: Little Mountain Sound Studios, Vancouver, BC
Producer: Bruce Fairbairn
Engineer: Bob Rock
Singles: "Bad Medicine," "Born to Be My Baby,"
"I'll Be There for You," "Lay Your Hands on Me," "Living in Sin"
Top chart positions: 1 (US, *Billboard*), 1 (UK)

Side one
1. "Lay Your Hands on Me" (Jon Bon Jovi, Richie Sambora; 6:01)
2. "Bad Medicine" (Bon Jovi, Sambora, Desmond Child; 5:16)
3. "Born to Be My Baby" (Bon Jovi, Sambora, Child; 4:40)
4. "Living in Sin" (Bon Jovi; 4:39)
5. "Blood on Blood" (Bon Jovi, Sambora, Child; 6:16)
Side two
6. "Homebound Train" (Bon Jovi, Sambora; 5:10)
7. "Wild Is the Wind" (Bon Jovi, Sambora, Child, Diane Warren; 5:08)
8. "Ride Cowboy Ride" (Captain Kidd, King of Swing; 1:25)
9. "Stick to Your Guns" (Bon Jovi, Sambora, Holly Knight; 4:45)
10. "I'll Be There for You" (Bon Jovi, Sambora; 5:46)
11. "99 in the Shade" (Bon Jovi, Sambora; 4:29)
12. "Love for Sale" (Bon Jovi, Sambora; 3:58)

Slippery cover was smart, as was shelving a 1985 photo shoot of Jon in bed with four topless women (even if he was single then). The sexual innuendo in most instances was more playful than crude. They had also hidden their excesses well from the masses.

    Entertainment journalist and former *Metal Edge* columnist Cheryl Hoahing recalls in our interview what originally drew her to the band back in 1986. "The music, and then the personalities, honestly," she assesses. "Jon was a good guy, and they were really friends at the time. They seemed like they were together. I love sex, drugs, and rock 'n' roll, but at the same time I'm not that way and they weren't either. I think that was a big selling point, especially when you're eleven years old and trying to get your parents to take you to a concert. My dad wouldn't take me to see Guns N' Roses, but he said, 'I'll take you to see that Bon Jovi, he's such a nice guy.'"

    The band celebrated the release of their fourth album with a huge première party in midtown Manhattan. "There was a party that Mercury Records threw at Roseland for the release of *New Jersey*," recalls Barry Fisch—former merchandising, sales, and then artist development for PolyGram from 1983 to 1992. "The whole of Roseland was turned into a boardwalk beach Jersey Shore setting, so there was hot dogs and popcorn and stuff like that. There is a video of that party somewhere. I remember the band came in and spray painted something on a piece of paper."

    New Jersey debuted at Number 8 on the Top 200 Albums chart in *Billboard*, and the next week began a month-long run at Number 1. It would eventually give birth to five Top 10 singles—the Number 1 songs "Bad Medicine" and "I'll Be There for You" along with "Born to Be My Baby," "Lay Your Hands on Me," and "Living in Sin"—the most ever for a hard rock album. The so-called Jersey Syndicate—bonded like blood brothers who kept family business to themselves—embarked on what would turn out to be a mammoth sixteen-month world tour beginning in October.

ABOVE: The boys at the *New Jersey* album release party at New York's iconic Roseland Ballroom on August 18, 1988. The Jersey Shore experience was recreated with beach umbrellas and hot dog vendors.

OPPOSITE: Jon showing off his patchwork jacket at a show at Giants Stadium in East Rutherford, New Jersey, in June 1989.

> **❝ I LIKED JON. HE WAS VERY FRIENDLY, HAD AN ENGAGING SMILE, AND HE KNEW HE WAS A CHARMER. AND HE WORKED IT. MORE POWER TO HIM. IT HELPED THE BAND GET AHEAD.❞**
>
> **Gerri Miller**, *Metal Edge* editor 1985–1998, December 2015

MAXIMUM OVERDRIVE

OPPOSITE AND ABOVE: The hard-rockin' and hard-workin' boys on the Jersey Syndicate tour.

OPPOSITE TOP: Jon and Richie rule the walkway hovering over the fans.

OPPOSITE BOTTOM: Tico laying down the beat.

ABOVE: David playing keys and singing harmony. The large-scale production was typical of arena shows of the decade, when bands had sets featuring things like a dragon (Dio), a robot (Judas Priest), and a giant spider (David Bowie).

MOSCOW MADNESS

THE MOSCOW PEACE MUSIC FESTIVAL WAS A MAJOR MUSIC EVENT BACK IN 1989, AT A TIME WHEN THE COLD WAR WAS BEGINNING TO THAW.

What better way to help spread some Western cheer to the country and help bridge the cultural gap than to send over some of America and Europe's biggest hard rock and metal artists to stir up the masses? Thus in August 1989, Cinderella, Scorpions, Skid Row, Mötley Crüe, Ozzy Osbourne, Bon Jovi, and drummer Jason Bonham flew over to Russia to join Russian acts Gorky Park, Nuance, and Brigada-S in a two-day concert event to promote peace and to help battle the drug war in Russia, with Western doctors coming over to offer some new therapy solutions. The event was promoted by Doc McGhee's Make a Difference Foundation (an anti-drug organization that he created following a conviction for drug smuggling in April 1988) alongside major Soviet promoter/musician Stas Namin and others.

Bon Jovi headlined both nights of the festival, and on the first night (August 12) Jon waded through the center of the crowd, escorted by Russian officers, wearing a Russian soldier's overcoat and jumping onstage. The group rocked out a shorter set than their usual arena-long act—it included "Lay Your Hands on Me," "Wanted Dead or Alive," and "Livin' on a Prayer"—and they ended with a big pyrotechnics finale. Some Western media were on hand to capture the spectacle, which was broadcast to nearly sixty countries. A video compilation directed by Wayne Isham was later released.

"I think he had the longest set," recalls Eddie Malluk. "People really liked Bon Jovi. I think they got the biggest response out of anybody. They played a really good set, and they had the biggest production."

Underneath the pomp and circumstance, the event itself was undermined by a few issues: many of the rockers got inebriated on the flight over, some later argued about who should go on when, and Doc McGhee (manager of Bon Jovi, Skid Row, and Mötley Crüe) found himself confronted by Crüe drummer Tommy Lee, who was incensed that Bon Jovi got the headlining slot and the fireworks. (Give peace a chance, guys!)

Russian rock journalist Vsevolod Baronin was a mechanical engineer and manager for the band Polygon at the time. He paints a different picture of the events in our interview. "First of all, there was no mention of Jon Bon Jovi in any Soviet media whatsoever until February 26, 1988," recalls Baronin, pointing out the limited music offerings to the Soviet public via press or radio at that time. (He says the first real rock festivals took place in Russia in May 1988.) Vsevolod asserts that Bon Jovi did not have a Russian following, and the September 1988 release of the album on the black market went by unnoticed. In December 1988, Russian state-run label Melodiya gave *New Jersey* and other Western albums proper Soviet releases. "Total sales [for Bon Jovi] in the next year and a half were estimated at about 4,500,000 all over the then USSR," reveals Baronin. So there was an audience after all; at least one hungry for Western rock music.

The festival finally came to Lenin Stadium in Luzhniki (Vsevolod asserts that the 100,000-capacity number was exaggerated and that the true number is 53,000; the *New York Times* reported 80,000). He recalls that "for August 12 there was no more than 40–45,000 people, maybe slightly less. It was one of the first rock events in Moscow when the black market didn't work at all—some of the 15-ruble tickets for standing [room seats] were

bought by black market traders the month previously, but on the day of the show you could buy those tickets from the same people for about 3 or 5 rubles, and without any problems! So, both events were clearly undersold."

The Russian journalist maintains that Bon Jovi, Cinderella, and Mötley Crüe were not anticipated the way that Ozzy Osbourne and Scorpions were. "Scorpions just stole the show," asserts Baronin. "From every other band, no doubt. They looked like any Russian metalhead's dream—especially dressed in their studs and striped spandex—and played like heroes, too. [Singer] Klaus Meine wrote the monster hit 'Wind of Change' directly under the impression of the event."

Bon Jovi got top billing, followed by an all-star jam of some of the evening's participants with drummer Jason Bonham. Although receiving second billing, Scorpions had the advantage with the audience. Former Scorpions drummer Herman Rarebell tells me that his band previously played five shows in St. Petersburg (then Leningrad) in April 1988, pulling in 20,000 people per night. (Five more sold-out Scorpions shows of the same size in Moscow at that time were canceled over fears of riots.)

"We were the first Western band to go there," says Rarebell. At the time of the Moscow Music Peace Festival in August 1989, he recalls telling Bon Jovi's singer: "'Jonny, listen, people know us here. In Russia they don't know you yet. It would be better if we play at the end and you play before us because I'm afraid if you don't do that, half the stadium will walk out.' That's exactly what happened. We stole the show—people saw us and left the stadium because they didn't know Jon Bon Jovi. He had no hits there. So for them it was new land. We already had "Still Lovin' You" at [the] Number 1 position in Russia. It would've been better if we had been playing at the end. At least that way Jon could've introduced himself properly [to Russian fans]."

Still, Bon Jovi did get behind the Iron Curtain and expose Soviet rockers to their own brand of Jersey style rock 'n' roll, for better or worse. However, due to various circumstances, they have never returned.

Many incredible things would happen along the way. The stage featured a raised walkway that allowed Jon to roam above and around the audience to get closer to them.

The Jersey Syndicate tour kicked off on Halloween in Dublin, Ireland, and journeyed through Europe throughout the fall, landing in Japan by New Year's Eve. The massive American trek included a sold-out and emotional homecoming show at Giants Stadium in East Rutherford, New Jersey, on June 11, 1989, with comedian Sam Kinison and rockers Billy Squier and Skid Row in support slots. Bon Jovi were now Garden State gods.

In the midst of all this craziness, two notable things happened. On March 30, 1989, Jon gave away his childhood home, a nice middle-class house, to Jay and Judy Frappier, a couple in their late twenties who won it through a highly publicized MTV contest inspired by his then-fourteen-year-old brother Matt. According to a report in the April 17, 1989 issue of *People* magazine, Jon was relocating his parents to a million-dollar home near his Rumson, New Jersey mansion.

Then Jon and Dorothea (who had reunited a year or so after they split in 1984) decided to elope. On April 29, 1989, during a brief break on the tour, the couple exchanged vows at the Graceland Wedding Chapel in Las Vegas, Nevada. Many friends and associates were reportedly shocked at first by the sudden marriage—one wonders whether his management was worried how his new unavailability might play with his female teen fans—but it soon blew over. And the marriage has lasted.

Over the summer, Bon Jovi flew to Moscow where they headlined the historic, two-day Moscow Peace Music Festival on August 12 and 13. More British and North American dates followed. Then on September 7, 1989, something magical happened on a smaller scale but with massive reverberations.

One of their most memorable performances that ever took place was not during a thunderous show on an arena or stadium stage but at a more modest venue for the 1989 MTV Music Video Awards. Jon and Richie chose to simply appear with two acoustic guitars and did purely acoustic renditions of "Livin' on a Prayer" and "Wanted Dead or Alive." Their intimate but powerful performances, vocal trade-offs, and spirited harmonies—not to mention some sweet Sambora soloing—electrified the crowd and has since been credited

ABOVE: Jon Bon Jovi and Richie Sambora's most famous TV performance included their acoustic rendition of "Wanted Dead or Alive" at the sixth Annual MTV Video Music Awards on September 6, 1989, at the Universal Amphitheater, in Los Angeles.

" IN THE LATE 1980S, JON AND THE BAND WERE THE SUBJECT OF FREQUENT TIRADES WITHIN THE METAL COMMUNITY. THEIR PLATINUM-SELLING CATCHY ROCK WAS AN ANATHEMA TO ALL THAT METALHEADS AND THRASH FANS IN PARTICULAR HELD DEAR—A SENTIMENT I LARGELY AGREED WITH. BUT THAT CHANGED WITH THEIR ACOUSTIC PERFORMANCE ON MTV OF 'WANTED DEAD OR ALIVE.' IT WAS RAW, NO BULLSHIT, COULDN'T BE FAKED, AND SHOWED US THAT THERE WAS SOME GRIT BEHIND THE GLITTER. WHILE WE DIDN'T RUN OUT AND BUY BON JOVI ALBUMS, WE COULDN'T STOP TALKING ABOUT THAT PERFORMANCE. THE RANTS AGAINST THEM SEEMED TO DECREASE EXPONENTIALLY OVERNIGHT. "

Alex Skolnick, guitarist for Testament and the Alex Skolnick Trio, January 2016

with inspiring MTV's popular *Unplugged* series, which began that year and runs still to this day. It also changed some minds about their true talent.

What had become crystal clear is that Jon and Richie made a good songwriting and stage team. That is not to diminish the contributions and presence of everyone else—this was a solid band of brothers—but the duo provided an interesting split appeal to their audience.

" RICHIE IS AND WAS THE YANG TO THE YIN. WITH THE BIGGEST ROCK BANDS IN THE WORLD IT'S NOT JUST THE SINGER—IT'S THE SINGER AND THE GUITARIST. YOU HAVE THE GUY IN THE FRONT WHO THE GIRLS LIKE AND THE GUY WITH THE GUITAR WHO THE BOYS LIKE. IT'S THE SAME WITH VAN HALEN, IT'S THE SAME WITH AEROSMITH, IT'S THE SAME WITH THE ROLLING STONES. RICHIE IS AN INCREDIBLE PLAYER, A GREAT SINGER, AND A GREAT GUY. "

Derek Shulman, February 2016

Accolades and reassessments aside, life on the road was beginning to wear on the band. After the MTV performance, they still had five more months of touring to go, and they had been on the road for a year already with few breaks. On the Biography Channel profile of Jon Bon Jovi in 2008, Doc McGhee admitted that he had been a bit of a slave driver in getting the band to remain in the public consciousness through incessant touring.

"Steroid shots had become like candy to me," Bon Jovi admitted on *Inside the Actor's Studio* in October 2009. "They were just like, bring it on, bring it on . . . until there was no voice left and I'm still getting jacked up. I don't look back on that period fondly." He was tired and sick from pushing himself to deliver onstage every night.

Bon Jovi tore through North America, Europe, Australia, and New Zealand, a few South American dates, and finally ended their global trek in Guadalajara, Mexico, on February 17, 1990, where they played two concerts on the same day while political demonstrations raged outside of the venue. Once the enervated ensemble finished their last show, they took five separate planes home without saying goodbye. They were burned out and needed to be alone. No one knew what the future held.

SPREADING THEIR SONGS

WHILE JON AND RICHIE WERE BUSY WORKING ON ORIGINAL MATERIAL FOR THE BAND, SOME OF THEIR OTHER TUNES ENDED UP MAKING THEIR WAY ONTO OTHER PEOPLE'S ALBUMS DURING THE LATE 1980S THROUGH EARLY 1990S.

During the touring craziness of 1987, the entire band managed to carve out a small amount of time to record two songs with Cher for her self-titled album, which was released in November of that year. The tunes—including the original "We All Sleep Alone" and the Sonny Bono-penned "Bang-Bang," which was originally a hit for her in 1966—were produced and arranged by the hitmaking Bon Jovi/Sambora/Child triumvirate, and Bon Jovi as a unit provided the musical backing, along with vocal support from Joe Lynn Turner, Michael Bolton, and others. "Bang-Bang" was a hard-rocking makeover of a song that was originally a Russian-flavored novelty folk tune.

That same year, the party anthem "Notorious," which was written in stages by Bon Jovi, Sambora, Todd Cerney, Paul Dean, and Mike Reno (the latter two from Loverboy), was recorded by that Canadian rock quintet and became a modest Top 40 hit from their 1987 album *Wildside*. Two years later, guitarist Paul Dean released his solo effort *Hard Core* following the breakup of Loverboy, and it included the mid-tempo rocker "Under the Gun" penned by Dean/Reno/Bon Jovi/Sambora.

In 1989, Cher recorded "Does Anybody Really Fall in Love Anymore?," an outtake from *New Jersey*. She dated Richie for a few months from late 1989 through mid-1990. Desmond Child produced that song and two other tracks, all of which featured future Bon Jovi bassist Hugh McDonald. (Guitarist/singer Kane Roberts would cover Cher's take on the tune for his 1991 album *Saints & Sinners*.) The year 1989 also saw Russian rockers Gorky Park, whom Jon had championed to get signed to Mercury, include the thoughtful Bon Jovi/Sambora rocker "Peace in Our Time" on their self-titled debut album. The song extended beyond typical Bon Jovi themes.

In 1990, Deborah Evans Price of *American Songwriter* reported that Paul Young, Ted Nugent, and Alice Cooper were among the artists soliciting material from the dynamic duo. Paul snagged the *New Jersey* leftover "Now and Forever" and Jon and Richie penned "If You Were in My Shoes" with Paul in Atlanta. Neither of those songs surfaced in Young's catalog.

Jon and Richie did learn about how songs can change once they leave the writer's stable. Jon cited the song "Notorious" as an example in their 1990 interview with Price for *American Songwriter*. "There's five writers credited on that song," he said. "There were only three in the room, me, Paul, and Richie. It was a rock song when it left my house. It turned into I don't know what when it got to Canada. They rewrote it lyrically. The only thing they kept was the chorus and a couple of the key lines in the lyric. . . . The song changed from an AC/DC vibe to Loverboy which was different. We were disappointed because the song reached the Top 40 but not much higher. It was a much better song we felt when it left us."

In the same interview, Richie discussed the art of balancing art and commerce in songwriting, saying, "You have to analyze the marketplace, visualize the direction where it's going to be by the time you finish your song and get it to an artist. That's the business side of it. The musical side of it is to always make sure it's from your heart and it comes from a pure place and it's something you believe in."

OPPOSITE: Singer and actress Cher riding the red carpet with Richie and Jon at the American Music Awards in 1988. She presented them with an award for Favorite Pop/Rock Group. Onstage, Jon said the band should give away the award to the critics "who said that Bon Jovi was a flash in the pan, who said that Bon Jovi was nothing." But he added that he was going to keep it at his house.

VI

SEPARATE WAYS

1990—1991

AFTER TAKING THE WORLD BY STORM OVER THE PREVIOUS THREE YEARS, THE BOYS IN BON JOVI GLEANED A NEW TWIST TO THE TERM "DIVIDE AND CONQUER." THEY MAY HAVE CONQUERED THE WORLD, BUT BY THE END THEY LAY DIVIDED AND NEEDED TIME TO RECOVER. FOR A TIME, JON BECAME CLAUSTROPHOBIC AS HE STRUGGLED TO RETURN TO A SENSE OF NORMALCY FOLLOWING THE LENGTHY TOUR. BUT NEITHER HE NOR HIS BANDMATES WOULD BURROW IN OBSCURITY AS MANY OF THEM PURSUED OUTSIDE PROJECTS TO EXPRESS THEMSELVES IN NEW WAYS.

In the spring of 1990, Jon was invited into the production of *Young Guns II* by friend Emilio Estevez, who was starring in the western movie sequel about Billy the Kid. The two had met through Emilio's fellow Brat Pack actor Ally Sheedy while she was dating Richie Sambora in 1988. Estevez wanted to use the acoustic version of the Bon Jovi anthem "Wanted Dead or Alive" for the film, but the singer felt it was not quite appropriate as some of the references were too modern, so while he was involved with the film in a cameo role (he gets shot within the first ten minutes, blink and you will miss it), he conjured up the lyrics to the song "Blaze of Glory."

Co-star Kiefer Sutherland witnessed this and later told *UNCUT* magazine in 2006, "When Jon joined the team for *Young Guns II*, we were all eating hamburgers in a diner and Jon was scribbling on this napkin for, say, six minutes. He declared he'd written 'Blaze of Glory,' which of course then went through the roof in the States. He later gave Emilio Estevez the napkin. We were munching burgers while he wrote a Number 1 song. . . . Made us feel stupid."

On top of penning that song, Jon came up with one more ("Billy Get Your Guns") that was used in the movie and eight more inspired by it. They would all comprise his first solo album *Blaze of Glory*, which also included a short orchestral track from the film's composer Alan Silvestri. His solo debut featured an impressive list of guest stars, including Little Richard, Jeff Beck, Elton John, Randy Jackson, Ratt guitarist Robbin Crosby (Jon sang backing vocals for one song on Ratt's *Detonator*, released in September 1990), and drummer Kenny Aronoff.

PAGE 86: Jon singing while wearing an anti-racism T-shirt. Throughout his career, the Bon Jovi frontman has been a supporter of many left-leaning causes and has always strived to offer a positive message in his music.

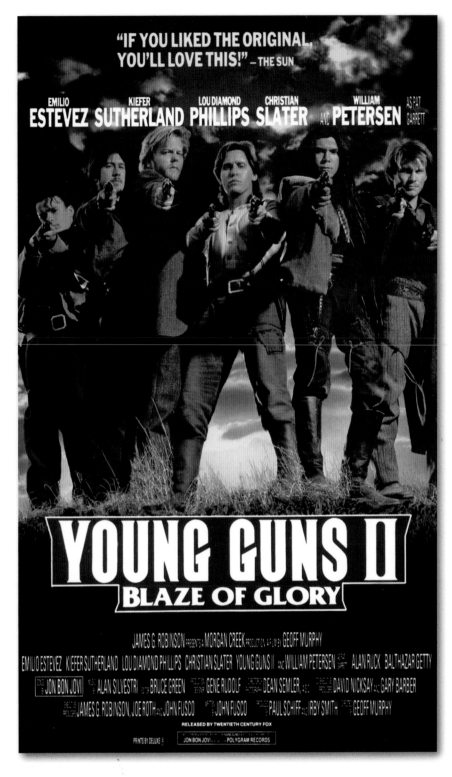

"IF YOU LIKED THE ORIGINAL, YOU'LL LOVE THIS!" — THE SUN

EMILIO **ESTEVEZ** KIEFER **SUTHERLAND** LOU DIAMOND **PHILLIPS** CHRISTIAN **SLATER** AND WILLIAM **PETERSEN** AS PAT GARRETT

YOUNG GUNS II
BLAZE OF GLORY

JAMES G. ROBINSON PRESENTS A MORGAN CREEK PRODUCTION A FILM BY GEOFF MURPHY

EMILIO ESTEVEZ KIEFER SUTHERLAND LOU DIAMOND PHILLIPS CHRISTIAN SLATER YOUNG GUNS II AND WILLIAM PETERSEN WITH ALAN RUCK BALTHAZAR GETTY

JON BON JOVI MUSIC BY ALAN SILVESTRI EDITED BY BRUCE GREEN PRODUCTION DESIGNER GENE RUDOLF DIRECTOR OF PHOTOGRAPHY DEAN SEMLER A.C.S. EXECUTIVE PRODUCERS DAVID NICKSAY AND GARY BARBER

PRODUCED BY JAMES G. ROBINSON, JOE ROTH AND JOHN FUSCO WRITTEN BY JOHN FUSCO CO-PRODUCER PAUL SCHIFF IRBY SMITH DIRECTED BY GEOFF MURPHY

RELEASED BY TWENTIETH CENTURY FOX

PRINTS BY DELUXE   YOUNG GUNS II JON BON JOVI   POLYGRAM RECORDS

89

A poster for *Young Guns II*, the western film around which Jon created his first solo album, *Blaze of Glory*. The film starred Emilio Estevez, Kiefer Sutherland, Lou Diamond Phillips, Christian Slater, and William Petersen, and it grossed over four times its $10 million budget. Jon's song "Blaze of Glory" nabbed the film's lone Oscar nomination for Best Original Song.

The bluesy album was a bit different from the four previous Bon Jovi albums, spanning the orchestral ballad "Santa Fe," the upbeat rocker "Never Say Die," and the gospel-flavored "Miracle." "Justice in the Barrel" was a standout with its atmospheric intro and soloing from Jeff Beck. Jon's friend Aldo Nova played guitar throughout the album.

As seen in *Blaze of Glory* behind the scenes video interviews, during the session with Jeff Beck, Jon turned to him after a solo take and suggested he play a section a little slower. Then apparently he thought better of it, as he pronounced that he couldn't tell Jeff Beck how to play the guitar!

Released within a week of *Young Guns II* and promoted by an epic Wayne Isham video with Jon playing in front of an abandoned drive-in installed atop a desert butte, *Blaze of Glory* became a hit for the singer-songwriter, who was working on his own for the first time since the formation of Bon Jovi. The album spawned four singles, three of which ("Blaze of Glory," "Miracle," and "Never Say Die") were turned into videos over a five-month period. Most

impressive of all about the two-million-selling effort was the fact that the title track, beyond being a Number 1 hit, later won the Golden Globe Award for Best Original Song and was nominated for Best Original Song by the Academy Awards and Best Male Rock Vocal Performance by the Grammy Awards. It also won Favorite Pop/Rock Single at the 1991 American Music Awards.

Upon winning the Golden Globe in early 1991, Jon, who commented in the interviews afterwards that he was shaking with nerves, remarked on the telecast, "I'd like to say I'm honored to be in the company of so many actors and actresses and directors and producers, and this isn't a pitch for me to get into the movie business." (That would come later.)

Rewinding to the spring of 1990, Richie was recuperating from the *New Jersey* tour at the seaside Malibu mansion of his then-girlfriend Cher. He invited his old bandmate Bruce Stephen Foster to visit and hang out with him, to bring him back to his Jersey roots. Once there, Bruce unintentionally sucked him back into songwriting.

"I'm sitting in this cliffside house of hers looking at Oscars and things, and I said to myself, 'If I don't come up with a hit song right here, I don't deserve to be a songwriter'," jokes Foster. "Richie heard me playing and said he had this idea for a song, and it was 'Trail of Broken Hearts.' We wound up working on it, and Cher came in from her rehearsal and heard us singing it. She was listening to it over and over for an hour, so when Richie took his break, she said 'I really like that thing you guys are doing.'"

She liked it so much that she convinced David Geffen, who ran the label she was on, to let her demo it as a possible song for the soundtrack to the Tom Cruise racing movie *Days of Thunder*. They recorded the demo with longtime Bon Jovi sound engineer Obie O'Brien in Philadelphia. Geffen loved it, and Cher recorded the anthemic pop tune "Trail of Broken Hearts" officially for the movie, which was released in late June 1990. Richie's old bandmate and also longtime songwriting partner, Tommy Marolda, who now lived in Los Angeles and Las Vegas, and had become a successful, Grammy-nominated producer, also contributed to that song, and worked on many other tunes with Richie, some of which would appear on the guitarist's first two solo albums. "We just holed up in Cher's house in Malibu and wrote away," recalls Marolda.

Richie also recorded a cover of Jimi Hendrix's "The Wind Cries Mary" for the soundtrack to the Andrew Dice Clay movie *The Adventures of Ford Fairlane*. It was the first of many

ABOVE: Jon rides across the desert in Moab, Utah. During the band's post-*New Jersey* hiatus, Jon took many motorcycle rides to clear his head.

OPPOSITE: Jon Bon Jovi holding his Golden Globe Award for Best Original Song in a Motion Picture, which he won at the forty-eighth Annual Golden Globe Awards at the Beverly Hilton Hotel in Beverly Hills, California, on January 19, 1991.

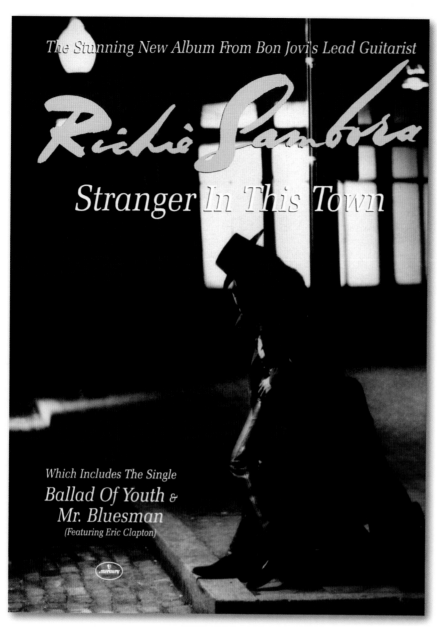

soundtrack songs that Sambora recorded between then and 2002, including cuts for *Zalman King's Red Shoe Diaries*, *Fire Down Below*, *Wild Wild West*, *On the Line*, and *The Banger Sisters*.

At the end of 1990, Doc McGhee united the band for a New Year's Eve show in Japan, but the time was not ripe for a reunion. As recounted in VH1's *Behind the Music*, journalist Lonn Friend and photographer Ross Halfin went there to uncover what might be going on within the Bon Jovi camp. Halfin admitted that Jon and Richie did not speak to each other during the ninety-minute photo shoot, and the tension was palpable. It was clear that that was where the main conflict in the band lay—they were equal songwriting partners but Jon got more of the attention—particularly in light of Richie's next project.

At the start of 1991, as Jon began developing his own record label Jambco, Richie began recording his first solo album *Stranger in This Town*, which included the participation of his bandmates David and Tico (as Bruce Foster notes, Bon Jovi's recent tensions came mainly from excessive touring) and iconic bassist Tony Levin. Dave co-wrote three of the tunes, including the trance-inducing ambient opener "Rest in Peace" which led into the haunting "Church of Desire." The album spanned a variety of moods, from the angst-ridden "Ballad of Youth" (co-written with Tommy Marolda) to the intense "Rosie" (a Bon Jovi/Sambora/Child/Diane Warren number) to a variety of slower, bluesier tunes, including "Mr. Bluesman," which featured a solo appearance from Richie's childhood idol Eric Clapton. The album impressively showcased the guitarist's multifaceted talents and was radically different from his work with Bon Jovi—a sharp contrast to the rowdier rock he had been playing for years.

ABOVE LEFT: An ad for Richie's first solo album *Stranger in This Town*. Ranked as a Top 40 album, it showed off his more soulful, bluesier side. It was a more marked contrast to the Bon Jovi sound than Jon's first solo release.

ABOVE RIGHT: A Richie Sambora promo necklace with a silver guitar pick was included with a promo-only edition of his first album, which also came with a bonus track and an interview disc.

THE LOW POINT IN OUR RELATIONSHIP CAME AT THE END OF 1989. ON TOP OF NUMBER ONE RECORDS, YOU'RE DEALING WITH YOUR FRIENDS CHANGING, AND YOUR LIFE CHANGING—AND IT'S ALL GOING BY SO QUICKLY. YOU'RE TRAVELING, YOU'RE DOING PRESS, AND JUST WORKING YOUR TAIL OFF. IN A THREE-YEAR PERIOD WE WERE ON THE ROAD FOR ALL BUT FIVE MONTHS, SO YOU CAN IMAGINE HOW BEAT UP WE WERE. THE WALLS WENT UP. WE HAD SO MANY BAD FEELINGS HIDDEN THAT IF SOMEONE DISAGREED WITH YOU, YOU DIDN'T DEAL WITH IT, YOU JUST STUCK IT BEHIND A WALL. WE KNEW WE HAD TO BREAK DOWN THOSE WALLS JUST BY TALKING AND AIRING OUR VIEWS. SO WE DID.

Richie Sambora to Nicholas Barber, the *Independent on Sunday*, January 7, 1995

The same could be said for David and Tico's performances, which showcased more subtlety than had been heard from them before.

Bruce co-wrote two songs on *Stranger*: "One Light Burning" (which began as a collaboration between Bruce and Tommy) and "The Answer," and was present while Richie recorded the vocals. "Richie had a very deep, spiritual side that really wasn't allowed to come to the surface as much as he would've liked with Bon Jovi," Foster explains to me, "and when he did his first solo album the spirituality part of it really came through. I remember just watching him do the vocals on things like 'One Light Burning' and 'The Answer,' and how he was approaching it almost like prayer. He was just so earnest with it."

Richie later told Bruce that "The Answer," a song about coping with the transition of death regardless of your spiritual belief system, became an elegy of sorts for people and that some people had said they wanted it played at their funeral. "Listening to 'The Answer' helped me through a death within my family, and I've recently found that 'One Light Burning' puts me in a nice place before I meditate," says journalist Gail Flug. "The album goes far deeper and is such a departure from anything Bon Jovi was doing at the time; perhaps that's why it did not do as well as it should. However, I think it did influence the band to be a little more edgy and less poppy." (Bruce says that "One Light Burning" was later played during an Olympic ceremony.)

Released in September 1991, *Stranger in This Town* became a Top 40 album, although it deserved wider exposure. That same year Richie also played guitar for and co-wrote two songs with Desmond Child for his solo album debut *Discipline*, which peaked at Number 74 on the Top 200. Tico also played drums on some of the tracks on Child's album.

Keyboardist Larry Fast, who had toured with Peter Gabriel during the 1980s and originally came to musical prominence in the 1970s with his pioneering electronic music project

LAUNCHING A LABEL

H AVING ALREADY CONQUERED THE ROCK WORLD WITH HIS BAND AND HIS FIRST SOLO PROJECT, JON BON JOVI SET HIS SIGHTS ON BECOMING A LABEL MOGUL IN 1991.

He certainly had displayed good judgment in picking bands that would become multi-platinum sellers. Jon helped Philadelphia rockers Cinderella get signed to Mercury in 1985, and he and Richie helped his old bandmate Dave "Snake" Sabo and his metal band Skid Row get signed to Atlantic in the late 1980s. Only Russian hard rockers Gorky Park, who landed at Mercury, failed to take off in America, but they did generate some international buzz which helped cement them as homeland heroes.

When he formed Jambco Records—the name referred to the first names of himself, his brothers Anthony and Matt (who were reportedly involved with the venture), and their last name—Jon set about releasing artists whom he liked and had a personal belief in. The two and ultimately only Jambco releases were *Pretty Blue World* by New York singer-songwriter Billy Falcon and *Blood on the Bricks* by his old friend Aldo Nova, who was staging a comeback with his first new album in six years.

Jon had followed Billy Falcon's career as the singer-songwriter built up a small following in the New York/New Jersey area. Billy had released six studio albums prior to his Jambco debut, starting in 1977 with *Burning Rose*. Known for his sensitive, insightful songwriting, Billy would become a major Bon Jovi songwriting collaborator down the line. With *Pretty Blue World*, he was gaining some wider exposure. Two videos, for "Power Windows" and "Heaven's Highest Hill," were released. The former song peaked at Number 35 on the Hot 100 Singles chart but the album failed to crack the Top 200 albums.

In the case of Aldo Nova, the Canadian rocker had not recorded new music since 1985, waiting out his contract because he did not like the terms. Seeking to draw him out of his dormancy, Jon invited Aldo onstage during the band's show at the Montreal Forum in June 1989.

"Once I got on stage and heard the roar of 20,000 people, it was over," Nova recalled to Joe Nichols on Canadian television show *The Performers* in 1992. "When I walked offstage I was electric. [Jon] looked at me and goes, 'What do you think?' I go, 'This is what I've wanted to do since I was a kid.'" So Jon invited him on the road for a week, and they started writing. Aldo recalled in the same interview that, "The chemistry was still there, and we got along great and wrote great stuff. We just kept going, and the next thing you know we had twenty songs."

When he started his label, Jon subsequently co-produced and co-wrote the songs for Aldo's fourth album *Blood on the Bricks*, imbuing his raucous energy into the mix. The album offered

high energy, bluesy hard rock that fitted in with Aldo's musical trajectory. Session musicians included bassist (and future *American Idol* judge) Randy Jackson and drummer Kenny Aronoff. The title track hit Number 14 on the Mainstream Rock Songs chart and the album peaked at Number 124. Munsey Ricci, then PolyGram Records' director of national metal promotion, worked radio promotion for the album and estimates sales were at least 300,000.

While both albums were passion projects for Jon, he needed to immerse himself in the business end of things while working on them. "He got to hang around the office a lot more," recalls Barry Fisch, former artist development for PolyGram at that time. "I remember seeing him often and getting in on meetings. I think part of it was an experience that he was looking to have, to learn how the business works from an inside the label point of view and not just from a band's or an artist's point of view. He probably thought that by gaining that traction he could apply it toward his own artistry or Bon Jovi the band."

Eddie Trunk also recalls that when he was offered a job at Jambco later in 1991, at the time there was only one employee at the label. "The guy said to me, 'Don't stress on this decision because when he gets back from this trip he is going to fold his label.'"

When Jon returned from the band's therapy trip to St. Thomas in October, he did indeed inform Eddie that the label was folding. Eddie recalls that Aldo Nova and Billy Falcon were both out on free radio tours that were "just hemorrhaging money. He definitely had a passion for some of those artists to the point that he signed them to this label, but he just couldn't get them going from a label standpoint and he folded that really quickly."

The venture was not a total loss. The business experience that Jon gained would undoubtedly help him when he started Bon Jovi Management to run the band's business affairs, which would continue until he hired Irving Azoff to take over the managerial reins in 2015.

> ❝ EVERY BAND HAS AN EVOLUTION, AND WHEN YOU'RE OUT ON TOUR WITH THE SAME GUYS, THEY'RE YOUR FAMILY, THEY'RE YOUR BROTHERS. YOU'RE OUT WITH THEM FOR MONTHS AT A POP, THEN YOU'RE IN THE STUDIO MAKING RECORDS. YOU GET ON EVERYBODY'S NERVES. I THINK THE BAND TOOK A LITTLE BIT OF A BREATHER JUST TO GET AWAY FROM EVERYBODY. I DON'T THINK EVERYBODY WAS REALLY TOO WORRIED ABOUT THE BAND BREAKING UP PER SE AS THEY WERE [LIKE] YOU GUYS HAVE TO MAKE ANOTHER RECORD. ❞

Munsey Ricci, president of Skateboard Marketing, February 2016

Synergy, was hired to bring some of his special sounds to Richie's record. Producer Neil Dorfsman, a friend of Larry, called him in.

"I remember him saying, 'Can you come in and help us get this more Peter Gabriel-esque or a broader sound that is a little different than what Bon Jovi does, but please be careful and don't step on anybody's toes. Don't offend anybody," Fast recalls to me. He was aware of Bon Jovi and unknowingly had many friends in common with the band's keyboardist. "I think David called me up a couple of nights before we were first recording just to introduce himself and he was just absolutely charming, humble, and a nice guy. He was actually apologetic about Bon Jovi, which just blew me away because I had an enormous amount of respect for what they had accomplished. I think he was looking at it more with my Peter Gabriel and electronic music connections and a certain niche which Bon Jovi wasn't part of, but which David certainly knew well and had a lot of respect for."

The two men hit it off and developed a strong personal bond, becoming adopted brothers in music. Over the coming year the duo would work on three movie soundtracks, two of which would be completed.

Bon Jovi's next fully assembled appearance occurred when they united to support Jon for a strong performance of "Blaze of Glory" at the Academy Awards ceremony on March 25, 1991.

Television and radio personality Eddie Trunk recalls that around mid-1991 Jon had discussed the possibility of him working for the Jambco label, and during one meeting, the topic shifted to something more serious. "At that point, Bon Jovi was in a really fractured state and he didn't know what was going to happen or the way things were going to go with the band," Trunk tells me. "Even then, there were questions about whether Richie would still be around. There was a period of time there before *Keep the Faith* where Jon and I would have conversations and he would bounce some things off of me. He would talk about the other guys in the band and asked me if I thought it would impact his draw if they weren't there because everybody knows Jon is the only one signed to the deal." While Eddie loves all the members, one potential loss stuck out the most. "We went down the list of people in the band, and when he got down to Richie, I said, 'No—Richie is the guy you really need. He's your right-hand guy, he's the other star in the band, he's your songwriting partner. I think that it's important that you have him at all times'."

It was clear that there were cracks in the facade. The band had still not come together to resolve their differences.

Jon commented in interviews that he was unhappy during that period, referring to it, as cited in the *Orlando Sentinel* on March 26, 1993, as his "gray summer" of drinking and depression. He also took a cross-country motorcycle trip that summer with Dorothea, Doc, and some friends to clear his head. In the fall, when their manager convinced the band to receive a Lifetime Achievement Award from MTV, all five members (along with director Wayne Isham) begrudgingly showed up, and after getting offstage, Jon bestowed his trophy onto a young lady he did not know.

Something had to be done. Dissatisfied with his managerial situation and feeling that Doc did not have a wider vision for his career, which included venturing further into movies, Jon fired him and formed his own management company. Then in October he chose to reunite his spiritually wounded musical brothers and go to St. Thomas, one of the Virgin Islands, where they met with a counselor to openly vent their frustrations and confront issues that had bothered them. A lot of anger and resentment had swelled up during the exhaustive *New Jersey* tour, but by coming clean the five members of Bon Jovi began to heal. They reunited onstage in 1991 for a Christmas charity benefit concert at the Count Basie Theatre in Red Bank, New Jersey. It has since become an annual tradition.

The wounds were mending, and by spring 1992, emotionally cleansed and physically recharged, the group headed back into the studio to see where they could journey next.

DAVID BRYAN: MOVIE COMPOSER

FTER BON JOVI TOOK A MUCH-NEEDED BREAK IN EARLY 1990 FOLLOWING THEIR RELENTLESS TOURING SCHEDULE, KEYBOARDIST DAVID BRYAN WANTED TO EXPLORE NEW VISTAS, AND MOVIE COMPOSING WAS A STEP INTO A BRAVE NEW WORLD.

Following his work on Richie's solo album, David's first stab at composing for movies was the 1992 horror film *Netherworld*, the filming and composing for which took place around the summer of 1991. (David married his high school sweetheart April McLean that August.)

Directed by David Schmoeller (whose previous work included *The Seduction* with Morgan Fairchild and *Puppet Master*, a cult classic that spawned a continuing franchise), *Netherworld* was a B-movie about a young man who inherits his late father's Louisiana estate and is soon haunted by his father's spirit, seeking to be resurrected through black magic. The film featured a flying stone hand that killed people. The keyboardist wrote and composed the score in conjunction with Larry Fast, and Edgar Winter contributed original blues tunes. The Bon Jovi member got to be a part of Winter's band and even cameoed with them in the film. However, *Netherworld* did not exactly set the world on fire.

"You could see the flying hand of Satan coming in and see the strings on the hand a little bit," recalled Bryan to me during an interview in March 2010. "It was pretty much a music video. That's when I was throwing everything up on the wall. I wanted to do a solo record, so I wrote songs on that, then I did an instrumental version of it. I tried to do soundtracks, and you have to start somewhere. I like to do it, I thought I was good at it."

With fifteen years of classical piano training under his belt and performing music that needed no lyrics to express emotion, David was qualified for soundtrack work. And he had tremendous respect for Larry Fast, who he had met while working on Richie's album. "Larry is a technical genius and one of my heroes," said Bryan. "I went and bought my first synthesizer. He built his first. There's a very big difference in that."

Fast had done some television scoring work, including Carl Sagan's *Cosmos* series, but wanted to gain a stronger foothold in the industry, and given their strong pairing and ability to trade off styles on Richie's solo album, he and David made for a natural fit. David being the keyboardist for Bon Jovi helped open the door initially. (David's name was on the soundtrack cover, "with Larry Fast" was in the booklet. Both men were credited in the movie.) "He was a couple of rungs up the Hollywood pecking order ladder when he went in," acknowledges Fast. "He was very gracious and we always planned to do this together, but I was a realist and I was very understanding that they wanted to put his name on it because they could use a Bon Jovi sticker. We worked it out very cooperatively. He was a great writing partner to work with."

Despite being a B-movie, *Netherworld* allowed the two men to combine their talents for a score that required both steamy New Orleans blues and ambient flourishes. "The piano and Southern improvization with the New Orleans feel was David," clarifies Fast. "I don't really do that very well. He does that really well. The dark orchestrations are my world. I definitely learned from him. He was really good for me in broadening a few of my horizons."

The duo worked on two other projects, the first being the 1992 HBO crime thriller *Conflict of Interest*, which featured "Judd Nelson wearing the worst makeup I've ever seen," jokes Fast. "That was more straight film scoring. Because this was the early 1990s and I was trying

OPPOSITE LEFT: The cover for the 1992 movie *Netherworld*, one of four film projects that David Bryan worked on with Larry Fast. The direct-to-video horror flick was put out by Full Moon Features, the company founded by Charles Band that specializes in B-movie sci-fi and horror releases including cult franchises like *Puppet Master*, *Subspecies*, and *Trancers*.

OPPOSITE RIGHT: A portrait of David in the studio during the recording sessions for *These Days*, taken on January 17, 1995. Later that year, the keyboardist would release his first solo album, *On a Full Moon*, which was produced by Larry Fast. That album was later reissued in 2000 as *Lunar Eclipse*, which featured two new tracks, "Second Chance" and "I Can Love," in place of two older ones as well as his vocal version of the Bon Jovi hit "In These Arms," which he co-wrote.

to absorb a lot of early techno, there were a lot of really harsh, metallic industrial sounds, particularly for this really nasty character that Judd Nelson played. But then there were a few romantic, quasi-interlude types of things, and David put together some piano pieces for that that were very pretty."

The twosome were also brought in as the backup team on *Highlander III: The Final Dimension* "because it turned out they were in a contract dispute with whoever had been doing scoring," says Fast. "It got resolved so we never really finished that. We actually started working on it and had sketches of things, then it kind of fell apart."

David's attention soon returned to the reunited Bon Jovi, which occupied more of his time, and the two drifted apart to different worlds, although Larry brought David in to play on some music for the small indie film *One Way Out* (which co-starred future *Orange Is the New Black* cast member Annie Golden), for which Larry was music supervisor in 1995. "I don't think the track made it into the score," says Fast. "And I kept seeing David into the 2000s when he would come to see the Tony Levin Band on tour mid-2000s."

Larry also produced David's first solo album, *On a Full Moon*, which was released in 1995. "I did a couple of pieces that had some very light synthesizer orchestrations to them," recalls Fast. "We did a few more pieces than we chose to use for the album." A re-recorded "Netherworld Waltz" made the cut.

VII

FAITH HEALERS

1992 — 1996

WHEN JON BON JOVI CUT HIS HAIR IN 1992, HE MUST HAVE IMAGINED IT WOULD DRAW SOME GASPS OF SURPRISE FROM LONGTIME FANS AND MEDIA TASTEMAKERS WHO HAD FERVENTLY FOLLOWED THE BAND THROUGHOUT THEIR METEORIC RISE TO STARDOM. BUT HE PROBABLY WOULD NOT HAVE GUESSED THAT ONCE HE SHEARED THE LAVISH LOCKS THAT HAD MADE MILLIONS OF WOMEN SWOON DOWN TO A STILL BUOYANT BUT SHOULDER-LENGTH CUT, THE NEWS WOULD HIT CNN. WHILE FLUFFY RED CARPET AND FASHION STORIES HAVE SADLY BECOME THE NORM TODAY, THIS WAS PRACTICALLY UNHEARD OF BACK THEN. ALEC JOHN SUCH AND TICO TORRES ALSO CUT THEIR HAIR, WHILE RICHIE SAMBORA RETAINED HIS LONGER MANE AND DAVID BRYAN KEPT HIS NATURALLY CURLY LOCKS, ALBEIT IN A CLEANER, TRIMMED SHAPE.

The makeover made sense. By the beginning of 1992, grunge rockers Nirvana, along with morose metallers-mistaken-for-grunge-rockers Alice in Chains and Soundgarden, had completely dismantled the glam rock and hair band hierarchy almost overnight, making them last decade's news fast. Bon Jovi would also retool their sound to keep pace with the times.

When the members of Bon Jovi reconvened in the spring to begin working on their fifth album, they returned to Vancouver, this time with the engineer of their two previous albums, Bob Rock, taking over as producer. Rock, who had scored big producing Mötley Crüe's *Dr. Feelgood* and Metallica's self-titled album, balanced the Jersey band's anthemic qualities with a nineties studio vibe, meaning drier sounds and far less booming reverb. Songwriter Desmond Child also co-authored several songs, two of which—the title track and "I'll Sleep When I'm Dead"—made the final cut and became hit singles.

Given all of the upheaval in their lives, principal songwriters Jon and Richie had bigger things on their minds than their usual lyrical fare. They had also grown through their life lessons and by benefit of their solo endeavors.

At least two albums' worth of material was recorded for *Keep the Faith*, and half of it surfaced on their box set twelve years later. The songs that made the cut focused on a sense of unease about the world and personal feelings of insecurity. Certainly, songs like the majestic "In These Arms" and the romantic ballad "Bed of Roses" revisited odes to love, but in a far more sophisticated and stylish way than ever before. Meanwhile, hedonistic rockers like "I'll Sleep When I'm Dead" and "Blame It on the Love of Rock & Roll" invoked the Bon Jovi of the 1980s. But when Jon addressed social discontent in "Keep the Faith," sang about "Fear" of change in a disenfranchised environment, and expressed the frustrations of workers in an oil town gone bust (the ten-minute epic "Dry County"), he and the band were digging a little deeper into darker territory. Their trademark optimism was tinged with some nagging doubts.

Bon Jovi had previously been easy critical fodder for major media outlets, and in November 1992 *Entertainment Weekly*'s David Browne wrote a cynical review of the album through the perspective of a "friend" who got laid and partied to 1980s Bon Jovi and couldn't comprehend their evolution. However, perhaps now they were changing some people's minds. At least David Bryan was featured on the cover of the February 1993 issue of *Keyboard* with the tag line, "Like It or Not, This Guy Can Play!"

KEEP THE FAITH ALBUM

Release date: November 3, 1992
Recording studio: Little Mountain Sound Studios, Vancouver, BC
Producer: Bob Rock
Engineers: Obie O'Brien, Gary Platt, Randy Staub
Singles: "Keep the Faith," "Bed of Roses," "In These Arms,"
"I'll Sleep When I'm Dead," "I Believe," "Dry County"
Top chart positions: 1 (UK), 5 (US, *Billboard*)

1. "I Believe" (Jon Bon Jovi; 5:49)
2. "Keep the Faith" (Bon Jovi, Richie Sambora, Desmond Child; 5:46)
3. "I'll Sleep When I'm Dead" (Bon Jovi, Sambora, Child; 4:42)
4. "In These Arms" (Bon Jovi, Sambora, David Bryan; 5:20)
5. "Bed of Roses" (Bon Jovi; 6:34)
6. "If I Was Your Mother" (Bon Jovi, Sambora; 4:27)
7. "Dry County" (Bon Jovi; 9:52)
8. "Woman in Love" (Bon Jovi; 3:48)
9. "Fear" (Bon Jovi; 3:07)
10. "I Want You" (Bon Jovi; 5:37)
11. "Blame It on the Love of Rock & Roll" (Bon Jovi, Sambora; 4:23)
12. "Little Bit of Soul" (Bon Jovi, Sambora; 5:44)
13. "Save a Prayer" (Bonus track in Japan and Europe)
    (Bon Jovi, Sambora; 5:57)
14. "Starting All Over Again" (Bonus track in Japan)
    (Bon Jovi, Sambora; 3:47)

Just prior to the album's November release, Bon Jovi played some warm-up club dates, including one at Fast Lane II in New Jersey in October, where a decade earlier John Bongiovi and the Wild Ones had headlined. As Gail Flug reported for *RAW* magazine, they mixed up originals, both new and classic, with covers of "With a Little Help from My Friends," "Shout," and "Kansas City" (a Leiber and Stoller tune that Richie had played in the past with Shark Frenzy).

Such eclecticism was further echoed in their *Unplugged* MTV special, released on video as *Keep the Faith—An Evening With Bon Jovi*, which was recorded at Astoria Kaufman Studios in Queens, New York. The group was on fire that night as they rocked out a mixture of acoustic and electric songs in the round to a throng of elated fans. Debuting new tunes like the title track along with hits including "Bad Medicine" and "Wanted Dead or Alive," Bon Jovi was in peak form, from Jon's singing and Tico's drumming to their dulcet vocal harmonies. They gave "Love for Sale" an Elvis vocal twist (uh-huh-huh), and rocked up the Animals' "We Gotta Get out of This Place." The members of Bon Jovi looked united, happy, and were acting as a Borg-like entity (in a good way). And Tico's passionate pounding explained why he was dubbed "The Hitman." Jon even slipped in a speech about the importance of voting in the next election without sounding preachy or biased.

Upon its release in November, *Keep the Faith* rocketed to Number 3, spawned a Top 10 hit ("Bed of Roses," which had a Spanish-language version called "Cama de Rosas" on some Latin American releases), two more Top 30 singles, and went double platinum in America, reportedly selling millions more overseas. Fans got an extra treat that holiday season, when Jon and model Cindy Crawford steamed up their TVs with the amorous video for "Please Come Home for Christmas," a cover of the Charles Brown tune from 1960 that Jon recorded for *A Very Special Christmas 2*. (Upon its 1994 reissue as a charity single in Europe, it shot into the Top 10 in the United Kingdom and Ireland.) During their year-long world tour, the

OPPOSITE: Jon showing off his cow-skull tattoo during a 1993 show in New York City.

PAGES 106-107: Bon Jovi deliver another passionate performance at Brendan Byrne Arena on February 20, 1993. Clockwise from top left: Jon, Richie, Tico, and David giving it their all.

THE DESMOND CHILD
PARTNERSHIP

◎ VER THE YEARS, JON AND RICHIE HAVE COLLABORATED WITH NUMEROUS SONGWRITERS, BUT THE ONE WITH WHOM THEY HAVE HAD THE MOST COMMERCIAL SUCCESS IS DESMOND CHILD—THE CUBAN-AMERICAN SONGWRITER, MUSICIAN, AND PRODUCER WHO WAS A POPULAR HITMAKER IN THE 1980S AND '90S AND CONTINUES TO COLLABORATE WITH MAJOR POP AND ROCK ARTISTS TODAY.

Many of his hits are ubiquitous in popular music: "I Was Made for Lovin' You" (KISS), "Crazy" (Aerosmith), "Livin' la Vida Loca" (Ricky Martin), and, of course, Bon Jovi's "Livin' on a Prayer."

When Desmond was approached to write with Jon and Richie for their seminal third album, they immediately began penning songs with mass commercial appeal that would become known the world over: "You Give Love a Bad Name," "Livin' on a Prayer," "Bad Medicine," and many others. Their songwriting partnership continues to this day, with the most recent Top 30 tune being "(You Want to) Make a Memory" from the 2007 album *Lost Highway*. Richie even recorded one of their collaborations on his first solo album, a rockin' tune called "Rosie," about a man who dreams of taking away a stripper he loves to a much better life.

Child has an ability to conjure everyman characters that people can relate to. He started his career in a quartet called Desmond Child and Rouge, which included singers Diana Grasselli, Myriam Valle, and Maria Vidal (the "Gina" of "Livin' on a Prayer"). In assessing the group's past success, *AllMusic*'s Alex Henderson believed that "their R&B-influenced pop-rock was so unique" and admired Child's ability to craft compelling stories about the streetwise characters populating Manhattan.

No doubt that everyman quality is something that Jon and Richie plugged into when they all began jamming in Richie's parents' basement in early 1986. At first, Richie thought that the verses to "You Give Love a Bad Name" were too Michael Jackson-ish. Child insisted he give them that heavy guitar chug so common in the eighties. Then it all clicked. On the first three Bon Jovi albums that Child contributed to, all but one of the nine tracks was turned into a single/video. Some of their songs got spun off to other artists or used as Bon Jovi B-sides.

While Jon and Richie would score successful songs on their own, and Jon would write many songs alone for the band in the 1990s, Child was an instrumental force in breaking them to the masses by serving up relatable songs with mass appeal. His genius would be tapped by many more artists down the line, including Ratt, Aerosmith, Joan Jett & the Blackhearts, Kelly Clarkson, Ricky Martin, and Selena Gomez.

OPPOSITE: A more recent photograph of Desmond Child. The songwriter and musician emerges from the the Music Box Theatre on the opening night of the Broadway show *La Bête*, on October 14, 2010.

FAITH HEALERS

"WE NEEDED TO FIND OURSELVES INDIVIDUALLY. THE BON JOVI SITUATION WAS EXTREMELY SUCCESSFUL, AND I WAS VERY HAPPY TO BE IN A BAND OF THAT STATURE, BUT THERE WAS ALMOST NOTHING LEFT TO WRITE ABOUT AT THAT POINT—WE WERE ALL JUST SO TIRED AND SO BURNED OUT. ALL WE WERE WRITING ABOUT WAS BEIN' ON THE ROAD AND BEIN' IN A HOTEL ROOM AND BEIN' LONELY AND TALKIN' TO YOUR GIRLFRIEND ON THE PHONE. THEY MISS YOU AND YOU MISS THEM—THAT WAS WHAT OUR LIVES WERE ABOUT AT THAT TIME. SO TO ACTUALLY TAKE A STEP BACK AND SEE WHAT WAS HAPPENING IN OUR LIVES GAVE US SOME MORE STUFF TO WRITE ABOUT. "

Richie Sambora to Steve Newton (earofnewt.com), the *Georgia Straight*, November 18, 1993

OPPOSITE: A 1990 shot of Jon wearing the famous Bon Jovi medallion that includes the double *S* from the *Slippery When Wet* cover. These necklaces are bequeathed to a select few who have proven their long-term loyalty to the band, including band members, family, and crew (see page 114).

PAGES 112–113: Jon basking in the adulation of fans on his band's *Keep the Faith* tour in 1993.

band played amphitheaters and arenas in America (Bob Rock's own group Rockhead opened many of those dates) and arenas and stadiums overseas, where their popularity was swelling. Bon Jovi headlined three nights at London's Wembley Arena and did multiple nights in venues outside of the United States. Jon was lucky that during a quick tour break he got to witness the birth of his daughter and first child, Stephanie Rose on May 31, 1993.

There was a three-month break at the beginning of 1994 before the group returned to making music. On March 10, 1994, April McLean gave birth to twins, Gabrielle Luna and Colton Moon, making David Bryan the second Bon Jovi father. Reinvigorated by the success of the tour and the warm reception by fans to the new material, Bon Jovi continued along their new musical trajectory. The rest of the boys got more of a break as Jon and Richie spent months working on material, and as usual demoing way more songs than they needed. Given that they required more time to complete the album—partly due, no doubt, to Jon having started acting in his film debut *Moonlight and Valentino*; he also recorded a cover of George Gershwin's "How Long Has This Been Going On?" with Beatles producer Sir George Martin for the tribute album *The Glory of Gershwin*—the group decided to fill the gap by recording two songs for a greatest hits album (and companion video collection) called *Cross Road*. One was the countryish "Someday I'll Be Saturday Night" and the other was the string-laden ballad "Always," a song that Jon had written for the 1993 movie *Romeo Is Bleeding* (it is name checked in the lyrics) but was pulled from that project when the singer was disappointed with the finished film.

Veteran rock producer Kevin Shirley served as engineer on the two new *Cross Road* songs. "It was good to work with them," says Shirley when we speak. "They were pretty straightforward sessions. Peter Collins was producing, and I think it was their first experience with Peter. I was very active in the actual recording. We used to go out at night to a place on Second Avenue in Nashville. It was just a lot of fun. I think Richie had just begun dating Heather [Locklear] at the time, so he was smitten and on the phone to her quite regularly."

Unlike the power ballads of the 1980s with their majestic, epic soloing, Richie's playing was understated on "Always." "I think we put Richie's guitar through a Leslie speaker to get that kind of wobbly sound," recalls Shirley. "[Journey guitarist] Neil Schon always said that they pinched the idea from him." Kevin felt that the band's chemistry was good at the time, and

ABOVE: Jon and Richie out on the town with their respective wives, Dorothea Hurley (at left) and Heather Locklear (right) in 1995. Richie and Heather would divorce in 2007.

adds, "That was at the time when they had the shadow bass player. They didn't have their regular bass player, they had their studio bass player."

Around the October release of *Cross Road*, bassist Alec John Such parted ways with the band. Over the summer, Alec had given a somewhat contentious interview to British journalist Dave Ling from *RAW* magazine about not recording on the band's next album, how he had been criticized by Jon about his bass playing, and how he wanted to jam with other people. He added that during their hiatus he had sustained injuries in a motorcycle accident that had made it difficult for him to pursue other musical activities. Naturally his comments made for a juicy story.

This breach of confidentiality was an issue for Bon Jovi, which as a band had a pact that they did not discuss personal business outside of their organization. During their wild 1980s heyday, their antics were not openly divulged to the press, nor were their personal issues. In the late 1980s they had begun giving out silver medallions, shaped like the Superman logo and featuring the double *S* logo from the *Slippery When Wet* cover, to people who had shown longtime loyalty to them, and it is a tradition that has continued.

Alec had opened up about internal strife, which may have led to his leaving the band. Some people contend that the real reason Alec was asked to leave was because he could not keep up with the demanding work pace. Rumors have

❜❜ A LOT OF THE WIVES AND GIRLFRIENDS OF OTHER BANDS, EVEN JUST THE 'FOR NOW' GIRLFRIENDS, YOU SAW THEM. . . . DOROTHEA, I NEVER SAW HER AROUND. WHEN RICHIE WAS MARRIED TO HEATHER, I NEVER SAW HER AT A CONCERT. I CAN'T REALLY THINK OF THEM HAVING WIVES AND GIRLFRIENDS AROUND. ❜❜

Gerri Miller, December 2015

THESE DAYS ALBUM

Release dates: June 27, 1995 (US), June 19, 1995 (Europe)
Recording studios: Sanctuary I in Woodstock, NY, and three separate studios in Los Angeles: One on One Studios, Ocean Way Recording, and A&M Studios
Producers: Peter Collins, Jon Bon Jovi, Richie Sambora
Singles: "This Ain't a Love Song," "Something for the Pain," "Lie to Me," "These Days," "Hey God"
Top chart positions: 1 (UK), 9 (US, *Billboard*)

1. "Hey God" (Bon Jovi, Sambora; 6:03)
2. "Something for the Pain" (Bon Jovi, Sambora, Desmond Child; 4:46)
3. "This Ain't a Love Song" (Bon Jovi, Sambora, Child; 5:06)
4. "These Days" (Bon Jovi, Sambora; 6:26)
5. "Lie to Me" (Bon Jovi, Sambora; 5:34)
6. "Damned" (Bon Jovi, Sambora; 4:35)
7. "My Guitar Lies Bleeding in My Arms" (Bon Jovi, Sambora; 6:10)
8. "(It's Hard) Letting You Go" (Bon Jovi; 5:50)
9. "Hearts Breaking Even" (Bon Jovi, Child; 5:05)
10. "Something to Believe In" (Bon Jovi; 5:25)
11. "If That's What It Takes" (Bon Jovi, Sambora; 5:17)
12. "Diamond Ring" (Bon Jovi, Sambora, Child; 3:46)
13. "All I Want Is Everything" (Bonus track on international versions) (Bon Jovi, Sambora; 5:18)
14. "Bitter Wine" (Bonus track on international versions) (Bon Jovi, Sambora; 4:36)

◀◀ I THINK THAT EVERYBODY THAT HAS EVER SLUNG A GUITAR, PAINTED A PICTURE, WROTE A MOVIE SCRIPT, OR WANTED TO MAKE SHOES WAKES UP EVERY DAY AND WANTS TO DO IT TO THE BEST OF THEIR ABILITY. HALF OF THE REBELLION IN BEING IN A ROCK BAND IS HAVING A CHIP ON YOUR SHOULDER! I THINK IT COMES NATURALLY WITH THE JOB DESCRIPTION. BEING CONTENTED WOULD BE BORING. ▶▶

Jon Bon Jovi to journalist Talia Soghomonian, November 6, 2009

persisted over the years that outside bass players (including Hugh McDonald) were hired for the studio sessions for the first five albums, but these have never been substantiated.

Regardless of the circumstances, Alec was gone. In a fall 1994 interview with late-night television talk show host Tom Snyder, Jon declared that there would be no official replacement for Alec and he stressed the importance of loyalty within the organization. Hugh McDonald took over on bass and has retained that position ever since, although he has never been named an official member of Bon Jovi.

THE MYSTERIOUS ALEC JOHN SUCH

RIGINAL BON JOVI BASSIST ALEX JOHN SUCH HAS BECOME AN ENIGMATIC FIGURE IN THEIR HISTORY. HE RODE WITH THEM TO THE TOP AS THEY TRANSFORMED FROM A HUNGRY YOUNG BAND TO ARENA SUPERSTARS OVER THE COURSE OF FOUR YEARS.

Despite Derek Shulman's initial doubts about his playing, Alec proved himself to be a good live bassist, backup singer, and dynamic performer. And as confirmed by Tico on a British television program, Alec was the one who truly lived the traditional rock 'n' roll lifestyle more than any other member of the band.

In that 1987 television interview, Alec told a British interviewer how he enjoyed the lifestyle that being in Bon Jovi afforded him. In the same interview, Alec admitted he had been arrested right after their Madison Square Garden gig opening for ZZ Top in September 1983 for possession of a handgun. He described how he had worn an unloaded antique pistol (for which bullets were no longer manufactured) as part of his onstage get-up and when he left the stage, the police had asked to question him about the weapon. He was released without charge, but it had been a scary experience.

However, Alec certainly recounted how he enjoyed the wild ride that the band embarked upon during the Decade of Decadence, and funnily enough, he and Tico being the older members looked more like the classic rock types, with cigarettes occasionally dangling from their mouths. They even joked during the British television interview that Tico was known for being the first one at the bar and the last one to leave. One might contend that a big reason Jon recruited Alec into the band in the first place was that his bad-boy image added a little visual flair to Bon Jovi in its early days.

Since Alec left the band, little has been seen or heard about the former Bon Jovi bassist. The band members did not go into much detail about his exit—outsiders have insinuated everything from poor performances to controversial interviews as the reasons—and despite having been the band's bassist ever since, Hugh McDonald still remains an unofficial successor. It has been reported that Alec and James Young of Styx co-managed the Chicago-based rock band 7th Heaven in the last years of the nineties, and that Alec also ran a motorcycle shop in the New York City area.

Alec John Such made one surprising final appearance in the music world when Bon Jovi invited him onstage to play "Wanted Dead or Alive," the final song of the final show of their 2001 tour, at the sold out Giants Stadium show on July 28. A fan captured the moment on video. Alec looked elated. He even bowed with the whole band at the end.

Since then, all has been quiet on the Alec John Such front.

OPPOSITE: Alec John Such hanging loose in 1994, the last year he would be in the band. He has maintained a very low profile since his departure.

Moving past their lineup woes, the Jersey Syndicate scored a smash hit with Jon's song "Always" and the October 1994 release of *Cross Road*. The album peaked at Number 8 and the song, which was promoted with a cheesy romantic video, rocketed to the top of the charts and stayed there for six months, making it one of their biggest songs ever. They played a few shows in December to promote it, including their annual Christmas show at the Count Basie Theatre in Red Bank, New Jersey.

These shows offered a break from the recording sessions for their sixth album, enough time for Richie to go to Paris to marry actress Heather Locklear on December 17. The recording sessions took place between October 1994 and March 1995 (Jon's first son Jesse James Louis arrived on February 19), once again with producer Peter Collins in the studio. Like *Keep the Faith*, *These Days* was an edgier, bluesier, funkier album than its 1980s predecessors, and it reflected their increasing maturity. It also featured a larger number of ballads, making it surprisingly subdued compared to the harder-edged *Keep the Faith*.

While Joan Osborne had been contemplating what if God were "One of Us," Bon Jovi's angst-ridden "Hey God" raged against the bad things that can happen to good, struggling people for no reason, as if God did not notice many of us. Similarly minded, "Something to Believe in" tackled waning religious faith. (Jon has been called a "lapsed Catholic" by some.) Even the love songs were generally tales of heartache, such as "This Ain't a Love Song" and "It's Hard Letting You Go." The album did end on a lyrical up note with the mellow "Diamond Ring"—one of four new Desmond Child collaborations.

These Days hit Number 9 in America and "Love Song" rose to Number 14 on the Top 100. Only one other song charted in the States and five singles/videos were released. In the United Kingdom, it was an unbridled success, racking up four Top 10 singles there. While

"FOR ME, BON JOVI WERE PART OF THE KINGS OF NEW JERSEY, DEPENDING UPON WHAT SCENE YOU WERE IN. YOU HAD FRANK SINATRA, WHICH WAS MY GRANDFATHER'S POP, YOU HAD BRUCE SPRINGSTEEN, BON JOVI. . . . THEY WERE THE ELDER STATESMEN OF THEIR MUSIC GENRES. BON JOVI WAS IN A UNIQUE POSITION, AND THEY HAD TO FOLLOW UP A HUGE RECORD WITH ANOTHER HUGE RECORD BECAUSE THERE JUST COULDN'T BE ANYTHING BUT THAT. IT'S A TOUGH SPOT TO BE IN."

Vinnie Fiorello, drummer for Less Than Jake, January 2016

OPPOSITE: Bon Jovi receiving commemorative plaques for platinum sales of *These Days* in Germany on February 26, 1996 in Hamburg.

five videos might seem excessive for an album that sold a million copies in America, *These Days* hit Number 1 in eleven countries, Number 1 on the European Albums Chart, and sold at least five million more copies overseas. Some Latin American releases included an alternate version of "This Ain't a Love Song" called "Como yo nader te ha amado." A two-disc European edition included the eight-song EP *Fields of Fire*, a highly sought-after item today, that included demos as well as covers of songs by Willie Nelson, Paul Simon, Bob Geldof, and others. Richie, David, and Tico each sang one cover.

"I loved *These Days*, and for me it was more for the lyrics," comments entertainment reporter Cheryl Hoahing in our interview. "There were really good lyrics. They were a lot about troubling times but not politically based troubling times. It was more about trouble with yourself, which is different than how he's trying to solve the world['s problems] now. There were a lot of sadder love songs that were very relatable on that album." An avid, longtime follower, Cheryl observed of fan reaction then, "When they started to change, everybody was talking about it, but the fans were still there."

Indeed, the throngs were in full force when Bon Jovi hit the road for another world tour, which began in Mumbai, India, on April 26, 1995, (two months *before* the album's release) and extended through to Helsinki, Finland, on July 19, 1996. While the long global trek sounded like another recipe for band burnout, they wisely took a four-month break at the start of 1996 and only did a few television appearances during that time. The band continued to play arena-sized venues in America, but they were playing more and more stadiums overseas, where about two-thirds of their concert dates took place. Many Americans do not realize how massive Bon Jovi had become on a global scale then. Their profile was not quite as high in America, but throughout the world they were becoming a household name. The video for "These Days" captured the spectacle of their overseas stadium shows, as did the subsequent *Live from London* concert DVD. Bon Jovi were so big in Europe in 1995 that hard rock superstars Van Halen, on their first European tour in over a decade, opened for *them*.

Yet while it seemed like the band was roaring ahead with a massively successful international career, it was actually headed for another hiatus, one that would last nearly four years. And when they returned, everyone was surprised by what happened next.

VIII

NEW
HORIZONS

1996—1999

AFTER A SUCCESSFUL PERIOD OF RENEWAL, THE MEMBERS OF BON JOVI TOOK A MUCH-NEEDED BREAK. DURING THE PREVIOUS FOUR YEARS, THEY HAD RELEASED TWO STUDIO ALBUMS, A GREATEST-HITS PACKAGE, AND TOURED THE WORLD TWICE OVER. THEY HAD REKINDLED THEIR COLLECTIVE MUSICAL PASSION AND PROVED THAT THEY WERE A FAR MORE SOPHISTICATED ENSEMBLE THAN THE POP METAL TAG THAT PEOPLE HAD PIGEONHOLED THEM WITH. AT THE SAME TIME, JON'S HANDLING OF THEIR BUSINESS AFFAIRS MEANT THE GROUP WAS SETTING MORE OF ITS OWN AGENDA.

It was time again to pursue some outside interests and live life. Tico married model Eva Herzigova in September 1996. His bandmates played "Always" during the couple's first dance. Then it was time for their honeymoon, after which Tico went off to play some golf and indulge in and rekindle his passion for painting and sculpture. Between 1996 and 1999, his work was displayed in fifteen different exhibitions across America.

Their frontman, meanwhile, was delving into acting and music. Jon's second solo album *Destination Anywhere* was actually born out of boredom while he was filming *The Leading Man* in London for three months during the fall of 1996.

Unlike Bon Jovi's often larger-than-life approach to rock, Jon's newest solo effort was a little more understated, rocking out on tunes like "Queen of New Orleans" and "Naked" while taking a mellower slant on tracks "It's Just Me" and "Little City." *Destination Anywhere* combined his bluesy sixties and seventies classic rock influences with nineties Brit pop sounds and electronic programming, giving it a modern flavor that made it harder to categorize. The intense "August 7, 4:15" was inspired by the murder of Katherine Korzilius, the six-year-old daughter of Bon Jovi's then-tour manager Paul Korzilius.

Despite its fresher sound and personal lyrics, *Destination Anywhere* did not grab fans the way his main band's music did. The album hit Number 31 in America, but none of the

PAGE 120: Jon on location in Manhattan for *Destination Anywhere: The Film* on April 13, 1997.

OPPOSITE, TOP: Jon accepting the award for Best International Group from Celine Dion at the Brit Awards in February 1996.

OPPOSITE, BOTTOM LEFT: Promotional photos of Jon for *The Leading Man*, which came out in 1996. It was a sinister turn for him onscreen.

OPPOSITE, BOTTOM RIGHT: Recently married Tico Torres and model Eva Herzigova out on the town on January 30, 1995.

NEW HORIZONS

JON BON JOVI stars as the charismatic actor Robin Grange in "THE LEADING MAN".
A BMG INDEPENDENTS release in association with Northern Arts Entertainment.

singles charted. A forty-minute short film of the same name, directed by Mark Pellington and starring Jon with Demi Moore, Annabella Sciorra, Kevin Bacon, and Whoopi Goldberg, weaved a tale of a man named Jon who is coping with his emotionally estranged wife (a nurse who cannot recover from the death of their daughter) and facing his mounting debts. An abandoned baby brought to her hospital may hold the key to helping them reassess their lives. The addition of the movie did not seem to keep the momentum of the album going, although the short film was a Top 20 seller on *Billboard*'s Top Music Videos chart. Jon embarked on twenty-five scattered dates for a solo tour that stretched between June 1997 and June 1998. Most of the shows were overseas, where he played arenas and stadiums, while the venues stateside were more modest. The greater success of the release overseas (where it sold over a million copies) showed how the Bon Jovi name had grown in stature outside of America. During this time, the singer pursued more acting work.

Meanwhile, Jon's right-hand man Richie had been hard at work on his second solo album *Undiscovered Soul*. It, too, represented a more intimate, mellower approach than his main band's music. Working with producer Don Was and songwriter Richard Supa—plus offering two tunes co-written with his old bandmate Tommy Marolda—the guitarist and singer crafted bluesy, soulful tunes that drew from his musical roots. He wrote thirty songs to whittle down to the dozen he presented on the album. When Richie was being interviewed on European talk show *V.I.P.*, host Catrina Skepper commented on his song "Hard Times Come Easy," and how that was a contrast to him being happy as the new father of a baby girl named Eva and with Bon Jovi doing well. Richie mused that he can write from different perspectives using his "emotional memory," allowing him to draw on different feelings and experiences throughout his life in his songwriting. He also talked about how he infused the music with a mix of rock 'n' roll, R&B, blues, ballads, and social commentary.

Undiscovered Soul was a low-key affair in the States, hitting Number 178 on the *Billboard* charts, with "Hard Times Come Easy" rising to Number 39 on the Mainstream Rock Songs

ABOVE: Jon Bon Jovi and Demi Moore on location for *Destination Anywhere: The Film*, April 4, 1997. Demi played Jon's wife in the short movie.

OPPOSITE: Richie promoting *Undiscovered Soul* at New York's China Club on May 7, 1998.

JON BON JOVI: SCREEN DREAM

AFTER HIS GOLDEN GLOBE AWARD WIN FOR THE *YOUNG GUNS II* ANTHEM "BLAZE OF GLORY," PLUS HIS FLEETING CAMEO APPEARANCE IN THE FILM, JON HAD BEEN BITTEN BY THE ACTING BUG.

For two years in the early nineties he studied acting under Harold Guskin in New York, spending $150 an hour to learn how to emote. He read classic plays and also continued writing songs for what would become the band's 1992 album *Keep the Faith*. "He really beat me up a lot," Jon recounted of Guskin on *Inside the Actor's Studio* in October 2009. "I loved that about it because you went in there with all this swagger as a rock 'n' roll singer, and in time I earned his trust."

The movie audition process initially proved nerve-wracking for him (he skipped out on the first one before even getting called in), but eventually he landed a supporting role in the 1995 romantic comedy *Moonlight and Valentino* as a housepainter who becomes the apple of a grieving widow's eye. The widow was Elizabeth Perkins. He extended his charm from the stage to the screen, offering a more subdued personality in his portrayal of the film's love interest.

After working on *Destination Anywhere*, Jon continued acting and taking on a variety of roles in a mixture of films, almost all independent releases that allowed him to push himself. "He takes his acting very seriously and picks his roles accordingly," says writer/director Roberto Benabib in our interview. "This naturally pulls him toward the more interesting projects made for less money."

Clearly, Jon sought integrity in his acting work, often taking on low-budget films that had no guarantee of success. Benabib's 1997 indie flick *Little City* was one of those special projects, a film about the romantic entanglements of six characters in San Francisco, in which the singer played a bartender who is a recovering alcoholic and who is sleeping with his best friend's girlfriend. "Jon read the script and wanted to play the role," says Benabib. "When his agent contacted me the answer was an immediate yes. I knew he could understand the character and play it in a very real and genuine way. He was also a dream to work with. It was a low-budget film and the amenities were, to say the least, threadbare. He was a great sport, went with the flow, and never complained." He even stayed in the same modest hotel as the cast and bonded with them.

Throughout the latter half of the nineties, Jon played numerous characters on screen. There was the manipulative American actor working in the British theater (*The Leading Man*), the blue-collar guy competing with his best friend over the high school sweetheart his buddy left behind (*No Looking Back*), the ex-con trying to live a clean life following prison (*Row Your Boat*), the alcoholic ex-boyfriend and failed father figure (*Pay It Forward*), and a suburban dad and pot dealer (*Homegrown*).

Jon got a bigger Hollywood break when he took on the role of a naval lieutenant in the World War II submarine thriller *U-571*. The intense underwater action film allowed the singer

to ramp up his often understated acting style and pull out his inner soldier. His character was Matthew McConaughey's best friend, and he appeared throughout the first half of the film before his character died in an explosion.

U-571 director Jonathan Mostow tells me that Jon's entry into that movie likely came through an agent pitch, and once he saw some of the singer's acting work and realized that he did not invoke his rock star persona on screen, he knew he could work within the ensemble cast. "We shot in Europe, most of it in Rome. We did the exteriors there," Mostow says to me. "It was a six-month shoot, and Jon showed up completely like an actor going to work. There was no entourage, he didn't bring one assistant, security, nothing. The first thing I did before we started shooting was put the actors in basic training for a couple of weeks, with a couple of guys from the navy walking them through drills and marching. Jon just fell in line with the rest of the cast and became one of the guys."

The successful *U-571* came out around the same time as Bon Jovi's *Crush* album, and with the band back in full swing, Jon had to put acting on the back burner. He would continue acting on occasion, including starring in nine episodes of *Ally McBeal* in 2002 as a hunky plumber named Victor who became the object of Ally's affection. But the romance did not last, and music commitments kept Jon from continuing on the show. (His take on how it should have ended emerged in the lyrics to "Open All Night," the closing track of Bon Jovi's 2002 album *Bounce*.) That same year, he starred as a methodical vampire hunter in *Vampires: Los Muertos*. Later roles have allowed Jon to be sinister (*Cry Wolf*), goofy (*National Lampoon's Pucked*), and sweet (*New Year's Eve*). One could joke that the latter film is a stretch because (spoiler alert) he plays a rock star willing to cancel a big tour to be with the woman he loves. His other television appearances have included *Sex and the City*, *30 Rock*, *Las Vegas*, and *The West Wing*.

Are there more roles on the horizon for Bon Jovi's perpetually busy frontman? Time will tell.

❝ I WAS TALKING TO MY PUBLISHER AND SAID IT'S NOT A BANKING DEAL; I WANT TO LEARN HOW TO DO THE ART. I WANT TO SIT DOWN WITH ALL OF YOUR WRITERS AND LEARN THE CRAFT OF SONGWRITING. THAT'S WHAT I DID. . . . I WORKED WITH TEN DIFFERENT SONGWRITERS AND LEARNED A LOT OF THINGS ABOUT CO-WRITING AND LEARNING HOW TO NOT BE ATTACHED TO YOUR IDEAS, AND THERE WERE A LOT OF VALUABLE LESSONS IN THERE. I LEARNED PEOPLE'S TRICKS, AND THEY LEARN YOUR TRICKS. ❞

David Bryan, March 2010

chart. Throughout 1998, Richie toured to support the album, playing North America, the United Kingdom, Australia, Japan, and Europe, mainly between May and July. True to his roots, he mixed solo originals and select Bon Jovi hits with covers by artists like the Beatles, the Temptations, Blind Faith, and the Allman Brothers. He was expressing himself in a different way than he did within Bon Jovi.

Jon's bandmate and childhood friend David also had other musical endeavors he wanted to pursue, although initially he faced an obstacle. Sometime after the *These Days* tour ended, the keyboardist was volunteering with Habitat for Humanity, building homes, when he accidentally cut off the tip of his index finger with a circular saw. "Doctors did a bunch of surgeries, and I could not play for a year, and I did rehab for a year," Bryan told Peter Manzi of *New Age Voice* in 2001. "I cut the nerve, so if I would even just touch my finger with a Q-tip™ the first year, it would feel like I slammed my whole hand in a car door. So they had to reset the nerve. That took a year of doing rehab on it three hours a day, five days a week. It was real torture, but now everything is good."

Getting back to music, David played on Jon's second solo album, and then turned his attention to trying to sell his own songs. "I always write one or two songs with the band; on the first couple of records I wrote more," David told me during an interview in March 2010. "I wrote a couple of songs and was looking for outlets to see what I could do, and I remember in 1998 I got signed to a publishing deal because I had written a song on the Bon Jovi record [*Keep the Faith*]. . . . I had ten really good songs, and one of them got covered, 'This Time' by Curtis Stigers [in 1995]. Clive Davis called me up and said it was the best song he heard all year, and he stopped Curtis's record and made him put it on it. And they loved the song, which was big."

More covers did not happen. As David noted, rock artists are expected to do their own material, whereas in country music using outside songwriters is more the norm. He grew frustrated with the fact that his manager could not sell the songs he had and he did not want to write more tunes that might simply languish in his personal vault. Then his manager finally suggested musicals, which David had not contemplated. He could get twenty songs covered eight times a week if a production was mounted.

OPPOSITE: David Bryan and Tico Torres during the 1998 Fairway to Heaven Golf Tournament in Las Vegas.

NEW HORIZONS

❝ ONE OF THE BEST THINGS I EVER SAW WAS WHEN I WAS ON A FAN CLUB TRIP IN '98. THEY HADN'T PLAYED FOR A WHILE, AND THE BAND WAS BOOKED FOR A ONE-OFF RADIO STATION SHOW IN FORT LAUDERDALE, FLORIDA. PART OF THE FAN CLUB TRIP INCLUDED WATCHING THE SOUND CHECK, AND IT WAS RUNNING LATE BECAUSE JON WAS MAKING SURE EVERYTHING WAS PERFECT. THEY STARTED LETTING PEOPLE INTO THE ARENA, AND HE FREAKED OUT AND MADE THE USHERS TAKE EVERYBODY OUT. HE SAID THIS WAS HIS SOUND CHECK AND HE DIDN'T WANT ANYONE THERE EXCEPT HIS FAN CLUB. THE REST OF THE PEOPLE HAD TO WAIT, AND THE SHOW WAS DELAYED BECAUSE OF US. THAT WAS THE BEST THING THAT I EVER SAW IN TERMS OF HOW JON TREATED HIS FANS. THERE WERE 200 OF US THAT WERE SUPPOSED TO BE THERE. ❞

Cheryl Hoahing, veteran news reporter, January 2016

"At the time he put me together with Frank Military," explained Bryan in the same interview. "John Titta was the publisher and Frank Military was an old Broadway guy who knew Sinatra and knew everybody because he was eighty years old at the time. He knew Francine Pascal, who was Michael Stewart's sister, and Michael Stewart wrote *Bye-Bye Birdie* and *Mack & Mabel*. He was huge. He was also in Sid Caesar's *Your Show of Shows*. He had passed away, and Francine had his whole world. She had a book series called *Sweet Valley High* that sold about 500 million copies in twenty years around the world. She knew Michael Price at Goodspeed [Opera House] up in Connecticut, and there was no rock 'n' roll at the time on Broadway in '98."

Thus David set out to write the music and lyrics to adapt part of the series for the stage, working in what he thought were hit choruses and "that [was the basic rock formula] for twenty-three songs," he told me in March 2010. "We got to a certain point where we had done a reading and they put about $30,000 into it. Everybody's opinion was, 'It's loud. It's too loud. Why do the songs repeat like that?' [I countered] 'It's not too loud, and it's rock 'n' roll. That's what a rock song does—it takes your emotions and is a simpler form than classical, but it is a highly complicated form of emotion.' So I got to certain point and then it stopped, and I sat around."

While that may have seemed like wasted effort, David learned a lot about the musical process. It would come in handy three years later when a musical script landed at his door that would change his life forever.

OPPOSITE: An enthusiastic Jon performing solo in Melbourne, Australia, in January 1997.

TICO TORRES:
SWAPPING STICKS

AS THE MAN BEHIND THE DRUM KIT, TICO DOES NOT GET THE SAME SHARE OF THE SPOTLIGHT AS HIS FRONTLINE COMPATRIOTS IN BON JOVI.

Even though he is known as the "Hitman," the Cuban-American drummer has other passions, notably golf and art. For over two decades, he has had his paintings exhibited in fine art galleries throughout the eastern United States as well as Colorado, Nevada, Tokyo, and London, and collectors of his work have included Michael Douglas, Bono, Arnold Palmer, Vanessa Williams, and dozens of others. He began painting at five years old but clearly took time away from it when his music career took off.

"Art, through my life with Bon Jovi, has always been prevalent," Torres told Thalo Artist Community in a 2011 video interview. "I would paint and really just give them as gifts to people or charities or stuff like that. It was a very private thing. I never showed my work to anybody until 1990 when we had a couple of years off. . . . It was weird. It was Thanksgiving, I was in New Jersey. I was sitting in a car and I saw a store that was closed full of art supplies. I said, 'You know what? I need to paint.' So I came back on Monday and went into a supply store and just started buying everything. I hibernated for six months. I lost 20–25 lbs, and I would just work. I lived in paint clothes and smoked cigarettes and pretty much internally went into my spiritual side, something I'd missed for so long."

In trading one form of art for another, Tico is also swapping sticks, in a manner of speaking. Music motivates him to paint. "Sometimes it's fun to have a white canvas and put some music on," remarked Torres in the same interview. "I mainly paint to classical music because of the lack of rhythm, because I'm a drummer. There's music in the flow of a brush. There's a melody to the color you use."

Many of Tico's paintings have been compared with German Expressionist works of the early twentieth century. Others are more abstract in nature. He feels his art is closest to Impressionism. "I see people in a way I guess that a camera doesn't, so I try to paint that," Torres said on *Inside the Actor's Studio* in October 2009. The drummer has also tried his hand at creating art in bronze, ceramics, and glass. According to a story in the *New York Daily News* on November 5, 1996, he created a series of sculptures "cast in bronze of the golf grips of greats like Arnold Palmer, Nick Faldo, and Greg Norman," wrote columnists A. J. Benza and Michael Lewittes. "Believe it or not, Torres isn't keeping a dime from the sale of these sculptures. He's donating the dough to his own foundation to benefit children."

ABOVE: Tico Torres on the green during the second round of the Alfred Dunhill Links Championship in Carnoustie, Scotland, in 2014. Tico says Willie Nelson got him into the game, which he has enjoyed playing ever since.

OPPOSITE: Tico displays his creativity off canvas and away from his sticks, as he sports an adult jacket that he designed for his latest Rock Star Baby collection presented at the Lupaco Concept Store in Seeshaupt, Germany, on May 10, 2016.

But by 1999, Bon Jovi sprung back into action. The group recorded the folksy number "Real Life" for the *EDtv* movie soundtrack, which was released in mid-March. The studio beckoned again. It had been almost four years since their last album, but what would they try next? At the time, boy bands, pop divas, and the rising tide of nü-metal ragers were the diametrically opposed but mutually driving forces of the music industry.

There was a plan to recapture the magic of their eighties pinnacle and come roaring back to the mainstream. That directive would initially be thwarted, but then a relatively unknown producer, a Swedish rocker turned pop mogul, and a stirring anthem would set the stage for a massive comeback that no one saw coming.

ABOVE: Richie and Jon braving the cold with a life-sized David Bryan cutout during the video shoot for "Real Life" in New York City on March 31, 1997.

OPPOSITE: Jon and Richie during the shooting of the "Real Life" video.

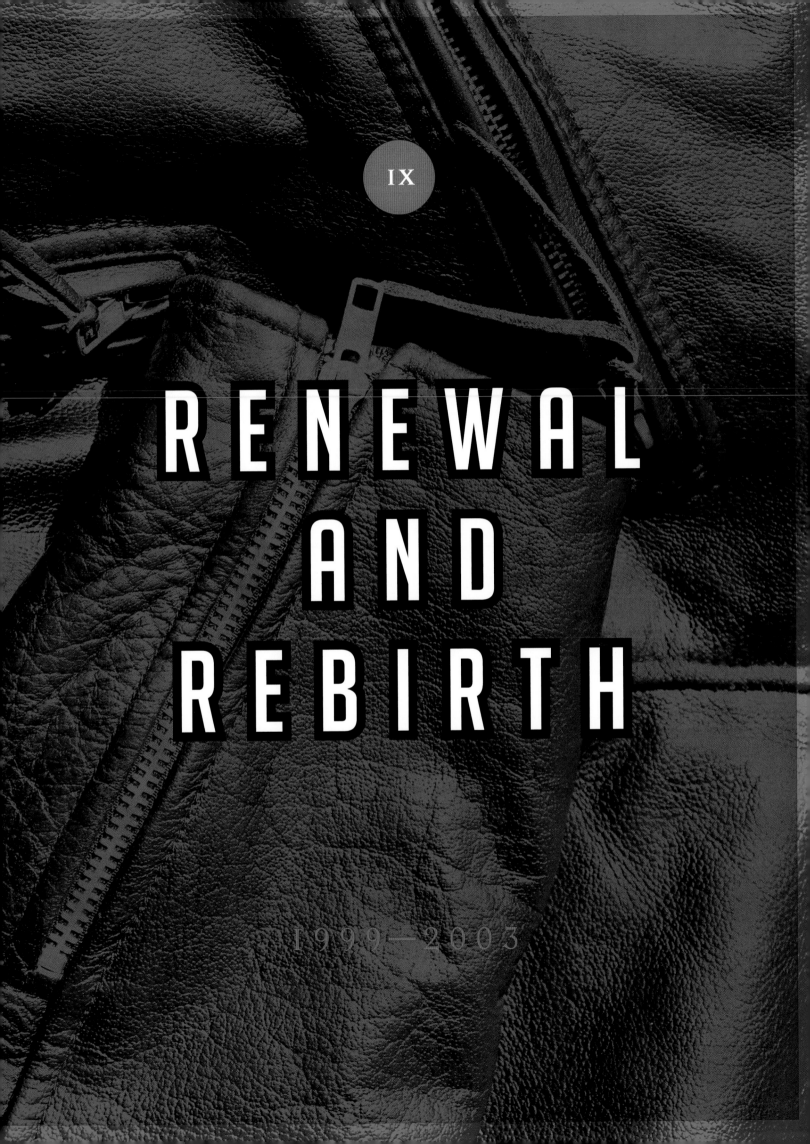

IX

RENEWAL AND REBIRTH

1999—2003

THE ORIGINAL CONCEPT FOR THE SEVENTH BON JOVI ALBUM WAS TO REUNITE THE BAND WITH PRODUCER BRUCE FAIRBAIRN AND ENGINEER BOB ROCK, PRESUMABLY TO RECAPTURE THE MAGIC OF THEIR EIGHTIES HEYDAY. BUT FATE CAN BE CRUEL, AND IN LATE MAY 1999, TWO WEEKS BEFORE THE DUO WAS TO JOURNEY TO NEW YORK TO CONVENE WITH THEIR NEW JERSEY COMPATRIOTS, FAIRBAIRN, WHO HAD BEEN MIXING THE YES ALBUM *THE LADDER SESSIONS*, DIED IN HIS HOME AT THE AGE OF FIFTY-ONE.

At that point, Jon decided that they would take a different path. He and the band met with various top-name producers at the time, but no one seemed quite right. The singer turned to A&R guru John Kalodner, a longtime ally and advisor to the group, to seek out a fresh face, someone not as well known, but with sparkling new ideas. Kalodner referred him to California-based Luke Ebbin, whose credits included pop punk and indie rock bands, and who was highly proficient working with loops and programming.

Luke journeyed to Jon's home studio in New Jersey to audition in an unusual way. The singer played the producer some demos and allowed him to pick one to work on. "I chose one of the songs that I knew would show my strong suit, which is orchestral arrangements, background vocal arrangements, programming, stuff like that," Ebbin explains to me. "I took it back to my studio, demoed it myself, and played everything on it and did all the background vocal arrangements and left the lead vocal for Jon to do. I brought my Pro Tools rig down there, and I said, 'You guys can just replace everything. You can just play off this demo.' They had never worked like that before, and they were pretty intrigued by the whole thing. A lot of the stuff that was on my demo ended up on the final track."

That song was "Save the World," and it made the album, which would ultimately be called *Crush*. (The original title was allegedly *Sex Sells*.) Luke confesses that while he knew some of their songs he was never a big fan of Bon Jovi, which allowed him to come in with a fresh perspective. He says the band were really open to ideas, making the creative process smooth and enjoyable. They were also reenergized after their hiatus.

PAGE 136: Jon showing solidarity with the NYPD by wearing an NYPD cap during the Concert for New York City at Madison Square Garden on October 20, 2001.

RENEWAL AND REBIRTH

Luke spent a lot of time writing with Jon and Richie and observing their process. "It was no different than pretty much any other duo's process," he says. "They were literally sitting in a room and banging their heads. Mostly [with] singers who are songwriters, you kind of let them roll with the lyrics obviously because they need to sell that, they need to feel it, and it needs to almost come from them. That's what it was like there. And then Richie was messing around with chords. I sat in a room and wrote with those guys and Desmond Child, and you could kind of see the wheels turning in everybody's head. Desmond was more jumping around with a gazillion ideas and you tried to harness the best ones coming out of him."

Both Jon and Richie brought guitars, and the frontman would occasionally sit behind the piano. Luke says that generally speaking Jon would come up with the seed of an idea that would get thrown around the room. "Richie is a good lyricist, too," notes Ebbin. "Jon trusted Richie to throw ideas off of, and Richie would grab it and tone it and throw it back at him." Jon would often come in with his own songs as well.

The writing and recording sessions were fruitful, with the group demoing thirty-five songs up to a rough mix. Another factor in this fruitful batch was the songwriting talent of Billy Falcon, the singer-songwriter whose album *Pretty Blue World* Jon had co-produced and released back in the Jambco days. The two were beginning a collaboration that would go on to produce dozens of songs. Falcon's more intimate songwriting style and reportedly laid-back demeanor made for a striking contrast to the more animated presence of Desmond Child. (On a side note, during this time, David and April's third child, Tyger Lily, was born on April 28, 2000.)

While "It's My Life" and "One Wild Night," the band and Desmond Child's lively rock response to Ricky Martin, offered the kind of energetic anthems one has to come to expect from Bon Jovi, the other tunes veered into different terrain. There was the Lennon-esque harmonies of "Say It Isn't So," the seventies glam grooves of "Captain Crash and the Beauty Queen from Mars," and the string-laden sweep of the ballad "Next 100 Years." According to Ebbin, "It's My Life"—the life-affirming anthem co-written with Swedish glam rocker turned

"THOSE RICHIE SAMBORA SOLOS ARE REALLY GREAT. HE DOES SOME TRICKY STUFF—HE'S PRETTY UNDERESTIMATED—BUT WHAT I THINK HE DOES REALLY WELL IS TELL A STORY. HIS SOLOS AREN'T ABOUT HIS CHOPS OR HIS SKILLS, LOOK HOW FAST I CAN GO, BUT HE REALLY TELLS A STORY WITH HIS GUITAR SOLOS."

Ruud Jolie, guitarist for Within Temptation, January 2016

pop mogul Max Martin—arrived halfway into the production of the album. Augmented by loops and electronics, this was a modern Bon Jovi that recognized its roots but moved forward. (Interestingly enough, it appears that Martin borrowed from his 1999 Backstreet Boys hit "Larger Than Life" for "It's My Life." A YouTube mash-up shows that, overlaid, the two tunes are remarkably similar in structure, rhythm, and chord progressions.)

The ultimate question now was: would fans embrace the new album?

When Less Than Jake drummer Vinnie Fiorello first learned of Bon Jovi's touring plans for 2000, "[Crush] hadn't come out and the first single 'It's My Life' hadn't come out yet," he explains. "We had been told that their campaign had approached other people to do the shows, and people passed. 'Bon Jovi is something of the past. They're never going to fill this. It's not going to happen.' Those other bands weren't feeling Bon Jovi."

Less Than Jake became plugged in to Bon Jovi through their then-manager Kevin Lyman (who founded and runs the annual Vans Warped Tour) and their then-booking agency CAA. Lyman told Bon Jovi's people of their love for metal and they got the support slot offer. "Immediately, without hesitation, we said absolutely do it," says Fiorello in our interview. Less Than Jake were Jersey boys and the headliners were among their icons.

When Crush arrived in June, "It's My Life" had already hit radio as well as VH1 and Fuse, who began playing it in regular rotation. Wayne Isham's signature over-the-top video showed a high school student rushing off to meet a girlfriend who is watching Bon Jovi play in a tunnel in Los Angeles. He hurtled through traffic, leapt off a bridge, rolled under a swerving semi, and jumped over cars to reach her and witness the spectacle. The catchy song, which made a lyrical nod to Tommy and Gina from "Livin' on a Prayer," was instantly infectious.

"I was in the studio with someone else and got a phone call from Richie Sambora," says Ebbin. "They were in London doing promotion because the record had just come out—and he said, 'We're number one,' and he named like fifteen countries. It was definitely a wild ride." Bon Jovi were happening in a big way again, and thanks to Ebbin's production and Isham's video they were reaching a young, newer generation of fans, expanding their appeal in a way most of their peers only dreamed of doing.

The world tour officially started in Japan in July, where the band remained hugely popular. The dates coincided with press promotion for the *U-571* film, so director Jonathan Mostow was

CRUSH ALBUM

Release date: June 13, 2000
Recording studio: Bon Jovi home studio, New Jersey
Producers: Luke Ebbin, Jon Bon Jovi, Richie Sambora
Singles: "It's My Life," "Say It Isn't So," "Thank You for Loving Me," "Save the World" (Promo)
Top chart positions: 1 (UK), 9 (US, *Billboard*)

1. "It's My Life" (Bon Jovi, Sambora, Max Martin; 3:44)
2. "Say It Isn't So" (Bon Jovi, Billy Falcon; 3:33)
3. "Thank You for Loving Me" (Bon Jovi, Sambora; 5:09)
4. "Two Story Town" (Bon Jovi, Sambora, Dean Grakal, Mark Hudson; 5:10)
5. "Next 100 Years" (Bon Jovi, Sambora; 6:19)
6. "Just Older" (Bon Jovi, Falcon; 4:29)
7. "Mystery Train" (Bon Jovi, Falcon; 5:14)
8. "Save the World" (Bon Jovi; 5:31)
9. "Captain Crash and the Beauty Queen from Mars" (Bon Jovi, Sambora; 4:31)
10. "She's a Mystery" (Bon Jovi, Peter Stuart, Greg Wells; 5:18)
11. "I Got the Girl" (Bon Jovi; 4:36)
12. "One Wild Night" (Bon Jovi, Sambora, Desmond Child; 4:18)
13. "I Could Make a Living Out of Lovin' You" (Bonus track) (Bon Jovi, Sambora, Falcon; 4:40)
14. "Neurotica" (Bonus track in Australia and Japan) (Bon Jovi, Sambora; 4:45)

in town. "We went to meet with them over at the Four Seasons and they had the entire floor of the hotel just for them," the director tells me. "They had a private elevator to the loading dock, the whole thing. We went out to dinner at this enormous restaurant that had been shut down for just us because it would just be too crazy. [Jon] just can't be [seen] in public in Japan."

By the time the month-long American tour launched in November, it was essentially sold out. Fiorello and his bandmates were definitely pleased with the wise choice they had made. While musically the ska-rock of Less Than Jake was quite divergent from Bon Jovi's arena-friendly sound, the openers relished the challenge and the drummer recalls that they made many new converts on the tour, even if people were there to see the headliner.

Vinnie remembers Jon visiting them before one show. "We were sitting in our [tiny] dressing room, and it was me and a couple of guys in the band, and one of them was taking a shower," the drummer says. "Jon comes in and says hello and introduces himself, which made me laugh because we're on tour with him. He came in humble, but at the same time he went into this thing about, 'I was on the stage a few nights ago and thinking you guys were back here. You're a young band and partying with a bunch of girls.' We laughed because that's not what the band was or the world that we were living in. The world wasn't a drug-addled party or cocaine-fueled orgy. That wasn't the world that people lived in anymore."

With every other day being free on the tour, Less Than Jake were playing smaller headlining dates, which impressed Jon. "He said, 'I saw that you guys are doing shows in between. Instead of just taking the day off you're doing it'," recalls Fiorello. "He gave us that big brother speech about how he was proud that we were working hard. We were sitting around blown away because this guy is paying attention to what we're doing and giving us a pep talk."

Vinnie recalls watching Bon Jovi each night and how every song was a sing-along and how the audience gave the band's energy back tenfold. "It was awesome to see," he says.

JON
BON
JOVI

DME TOKYO
DOME NAGOYA
DOME FUKUOKA
DOME OSAKA
NA TURKU
ARENA HELSINKI
AVIUM GOTHENBURG
TOCKHOLM
GEORG-MELCHES-STADION ESSEN
SUDWESTSTADION LUDWIGSHAFEN
A1 RING ZELTWEG
FESTWEISE LEIPZIG
WEMBLEY STADIUM LONDON
GATESHEAD STADIUM NEWCASTLE
BRITANNIA STADIUM STOKE
RDS DUBLIN
HIPPODROME WELLINGTON OSTEND
LETZIGRUND STADIUM ZURICH
GELREDOME ARNHEM
WESERSTADION BREMEN
WALDBUHNE BERLIN
ZEPPELINFELD NURENBERG
ARENA FESTA DELLA UNITA MODENA

"That was a band at the top of their game. They were professionals. It was everything that you would think that a band that had huge hits would be and do. Every song that was there felt fresh and fun, and the energy that people were giving off when they were playing was awesome."

Crush was a massively successful comeback—double platinum in America with millions more sold overseas. Bon Jovi played thirty-nine dates in arenas and stadiums in North America, Europe, and Japan. The tour was extended in 2001 with fifty-four more dates between March and July, culminating in two sold-out shows at Giants Stadium in their home state that grossed a whopping $6.3 million. They were also good sports in allowing themselves to be interrogated by Conan O'Brien's irreverent canine reporter Triumph the Insult Comic Dog, who covered one of the shows and mocked their middle-aged fans, perceived stereotypes of the band, and made teasing Springsteen comparisons. They even allowed him onstage to mangle "You Give Love a Bad Name." (Although it is not clear whether that was a sound check moment or an actual concert appearance.)

The *Crush* clincher? The band finally landed their first two Grammy Award nominations: Best Rock Performance by a Duo or Group with Vocal ("It's My Life") and Best Rock Album (*Crush*). They did not win either, but the recognition was overdue.

The second half of the tour was renamed the One Wild Night Tour to tie in with the live album release *One Wild Night Live: 1985–2001*, which featured a more slide guitar-heavy remix of the titular song overseen by Desmond Child in Miami. The video featured an appropriately hedonistic club scene where the band performed.

Following the tour, the members of Bon Jovi took a break (on May 16, Jon received an honorary doctorate in humanities and gave the commencement address at Monmouth University), but they were suddenly called back to action in a way they could not have

ABOVE: Bon Jovi's frontman in wise-guy mode on a T-shirt from the *Crush* tour.

ABOVE: Jon Bon Jovi shares his mic with an NYPD officer, and the stage with the Who's Roger Daltrey and Sheryl Crow, during the Concert for New York City on October 20, 2001.

foreseen. Following the horrific terrorist attacks on the World Trade Center on September 11, 2001, Bon Jovi played numerous benefit concerts to help families of victims in the attacks. Monmouth County in New Jersey reportedly lost a large number of rescue personnel and citizens, thus the group played several local concerts. They finished with their three-song appearance at the Concert for New York City on October 20, 2001—appearing alongside artists like the Who, Bruce Springsteen, Elton John, and Paul McCartney.

The following month they began work on their next album, *Bounce*, which certainly had the specter of 9/11 hanging over it, resulting in heavy and engaging tracks like "Undivided," "Everyday," "Love Me Back to Life," and the title track. In parts, this may be the heaviest album the band has ever produced, even more so than their late eighties work. Ebbin says the heavier approach—which was more focused on straight-ahead grooves and eschewed long or even any guitar solos at all—was deliberate.

▌▌ WE WERE UP AT MY HOUSE FOR MONTHS BANGING OUT [*BOUNCE*] DEMOS, AND WE PROBABLY DID TWENTY OR THIRTY OF THOSE. ▐▐

Luke Ebbin, producer and songwriter, January 2016

Because Jon was appearing in *Ally McBeal* for a nine-episode run, Luke moved out to Los Angeles to work on the record.

Some of the 9/11-related tracks ended up not making the final cut. These songs—"Still Standing" and "Another Reason to Believe"—appeared as bonus tracks on the "Everyday" CD singles released in Europe.

A new songwriting partner entered the mix with *Bounce*—a Swedish producer/songwriter by the name of Andreas Carlsson, who had learned about melody from Max Martin and lyric writing from Desmond Child, and who at the time had been working with

PROVIDING RELIEF THROUGH THEIR MUSIC

THE MEMBERS OF BON JOVI HAVE ALWAYS BEEN ACTIVE IN CHARITY CAUSES, AND WHEN THEY WERE ASKED TO HELP PEOPLE AFTER THE DESTRUCTIVE TERRORIST ATTACKS ON THE WORLD TRADE CENTER ON 9/11, THEY SPRANG INTO ACTION.

Jon and Richie performed "Livin' on a Prayer" acoustically for the *America: A Tribute to Heroes* telethon. Jon and David performed together at the Twin Towers Relief Benefit at the Stone Pony in Asbury Park, New Jersey. Jon, Bruce Springsteen, and Joan Jett appeared at the Count Basie Theatre in Red Bank for the Alliance of Neighbors of Monmouth County. And, of course, the group performed a memorable set at the Concert for New York City at Madison Square Garden.

The relief efforts have not stopped there. Since then, the band has lent their time with performances at events including Live 8 in Philadelphia in 2005 and the Concert for Sandy Relief on December 12, 2012. Coinciding with the twentieth anniversary of Live Aid, Live 8 raised tens of millions of dollars to fight poverty globally. The Sandy concert was organized to raise money for victims of Hurricane Sandy in New York and New Jersey, and Jon got to perform and trade vocals with his childhood idol Bruce Springsteen on Bon Jovi's country crossover hit "Who Says You Can't Go Home." The duo had shared a stage before, but this was the most high-profile instance. No longer was the Jersey rocker a kid who got lucky when Bruce jumped onstage. They were now united in music and by a cause.

The band also performed as part of the Stand Up for a Cure concert series in 2008 to raise funds and awareness for lung cancer research at the Memorial Sloan-Kettering Cancer Center in New York. It was a year after Richie's father had passed away from cancer. Other participants in the series included Jerry Seinfeld, Brian Wilson, and Andrea Bocelli. In July 2014, Jon Bon Jovi played a benefit concert, with his solo band the Kings of Suburbia, for the Parker Family Health Center at the Count Basie Theatre.

Long before 2001, Bon Jovi the band and the singer had been involved in charity causes, from their annual Christmas shows to benefit local food banks and women's shelters, to Jon's involvement in the Rock for the Rainforest concert series at Carnegie Hall back in 1995. Jon's philanthropic work in particular grew throughout the last decade and has been making headlines in recent years. He has performed numerous solo charity shows since 2014.

ABOVE: Bon Jovi onstage in Philadelphia during the international, multistage Live 8 concert event on July 2, 2005.

RIGHT: A poster promoting the 12-12-12 Concert for Sandy Relief, one of many benefit shows that the band has played at throughout their career.

12|12|12

THE CONCERT FOR SANDY RELIEF
TO BENEFIT THE ROBIN HOOD RELIEF FUND
MADISON SQUARE GARDEN
PRESENTED BY CHASE ◆

BON JOVI • ERIC CLAPTON • DAVE GROHL • BILLY JOEL • ALICIA KEYS
CHRIS MARTIN • BRUCE SPRINGSTEEN & THE E STREET BAND
EDDIE VEDDER • ROGER WATERS • KANYE WEST • THE WHO
PAUL McCARTNEY • PLUS MORE ARTISTS TO BE ANNOUNCED!

WITH SUPPORT FROM:
Lightpath   Samsung GALAXY   StateFarm   Time Warner Cable   verizon foundation

#121212CONCERT   121212concert.org

BOUNCE ALBUM

Release date: October 8, 2002
Recording studio: Sanctuary II Studio, New Jersey
Producers: Luke Ebbin, Jon Bon Jovi, Richie Sambora, Desmond
Child, Andreas Carlsson
Singles: "Everyday," "Misunderstood," "All About Lovin' You,"
"Bounce," "The Distance"
Top chart positions: 2 (US, *Billboard*), 2 (UK)

1. "Undivided" (Bon Jovi, Sambora, Billy Falcon; 3:53)
2. "Everyday" (Bon Jovi, Sambora, Andreas Carlsson; 3:00)
3. "The Distance" (Bon Jovi, Sambora, Desmond Child; 4:48)
4. "Joey" (Bon Jovi, Sambora; 4:54)
5. "Misunderstood" (Bon Jovi, Sambora, Carlsson, Child; 3:30)
6. "All About Lovin' You" (Bon Jovi, Sambora, Carlsson, Child; 3:46)
7. "Hook Me Up" (Bon Jovi, Sambora, Carlsson, Child; 3:54)
8. "Right Side of Wrong" (Bon Jovi; 5:50)
9. "Love Me Back to Life" (Bon Jovi, Sambora; 4:09)
10. "You Had Me from Hello" (Bon Jovi, Sambora, Carlsson; 3:49)
11. "Bounce" (Bon Jovi, Sambora, Falcon; 3:11)
12. "Open All Night" (Bon Jovi, Sambora; 4:22)
13. "No Regrets" (Japan bonus track) (Bon Jovi; 4:02)
14. "Postcards from the Wasteland" (Japan bonus track)
    (Bon Jovi; 4:25)

Britney Spears, Backstreet Boys, and NSYNC. The band members journeyed to his country to work on songs for the album, five of which made the cut, including lead single "Everyday." The finished tracks for the album were cut at Sanctuary Sound II, the new home studio at Jon's new, French chateau-like abode in New Jersey. (During this time, Jon's second son, Jacob Hurley Bongiovi, was born on May 7, 2002.)

Of Luke's production approach, Tico Torres told Billy Amendola of *Modern Drummer* in 2002: "He's a young guy, hip to computers, so he naturally leaned in that direction for *Crush*. Whatever loops he would come up with I'd record and make a new loop out of that. That's kind of nice, because you're using the technology to enhance your music, instead of creating around it. Thank God we've never gone in the direction where it demands it. I wouldn't have minded a couple more loops in there this time, though."

Although it had the highest American debut in the band's history, instantly peaking at Number 2 upon its October release and entering the Top 5 in fifteen other countries, *Bounce* was not quite as successful as *Crush*. The album was a better release than its predecessor, but as Ebbin notes, "It didn't sell [as well] because it didn't have a big hit single," which is a little ironic given Carlsson's involvement. It was the first Bon Jovi album since *Slippery When Wet* not to go platinum in the States.

The *Bounce* tour, however, was a bigger success than the *Crush* trek—eighty-three shows over eight months across four continents, once again wrapping up with two massive shows at

OPPOSITE: Richie and Jon exuberantly rock London's Hyde Park during the *Bounce* tour on June 28, 2003.

▶▶ I THINK THE WHOLE IDEA OF THAT RECORD WAS THIS RESPONSE TO 9/11 WHERE THERE WAS A LOT OF ANGER AND DISILLUSIONMENT. IT WAS DELIBERATELY MADE THAT WAY. I DON'T THINK THOSE WORDS WERE EVER SPOKEN, BUT I THINK WE UNDERSTOOD THAT'S WHAT THE APPROACH WAS. ▶▶

Luke Ebbin, January 2016

❰❰I WILL GO ON RECORD AS SAYING TICO IS HANDS DOWN THE MOST UNDERRATED ROCK 'N' ROLL DRUMMER OF ALL TIME. HE IS SUCH AN INCREDIBLE DRUMMER. WHILE I WAS DEMOING 'SAVE THE WORLD' I'M LISTENING TO HIM PLAYING AND THINKING, 'THIS GUY IS INSANE. HIS FEEL IS INCREDIBLE.' ALTHOUGH THAT'S STRAIGHT ON AHEAD AND IT'S FOUR-ON-THE-FLOOR ROCK 'N' ROLL, HE STILL FINDS THE SHAKE IN BETWEEN NOTES. I LOVE LISTENING TO HIM PLAY. ❱❱

Luke Ebbin, January 2016

PAGE 149: An exuberant Tico bashing those skins. This is a latter-day shot of the "Hitman" in action at a BBC Radio Theatre gig in London, on November 3, 2009.

OPPOSITE: Jon feeling triumphant at the final show of the group's *Bounce* tour at Giants Stadium on August 8, 2003.

ABOVE: Bon Jovi perform during halftime at the Giants vs. 49ers game at Giants Stadium on September 5, 2002. Prior to the performance, the group played in front of 750,000 people in Times Square, then flew by helicopter to the game.

Giants Stadium. On September 5, about a month prior to the album's release, Bon Jovi kicked off the 2002 NFL season by commandeering a stage in the middle of Times Square to play for approximately 750,000 fans, including a strong female throng that spanned at least two generations. They then flew across the river to Giants Stadium to perform at the halftime show of the season's opening game, the New York Giants versus the San Francisco 49ers. The group also performed "It's My Life" and "Everyday" at an NFL halftime show in Detroit in 2002. Being a football fan, Jon was undoubtedly stoked.

Even if *Bounce* was not as hit-laden as *Crush*, the Bon Jovi machine was moving full steam ahead, proving that their revival was no fluke. The success of their first two twenty-first century albums could be attributed to the fact that they were open to working with different people, even those who were newer to the rock world such as Luke Ebbin, who imbued the band with extra edginess on *Bounce*.

"First of all, the thing that I came to realize when I was working with them is that these guys are a lot more sophisticated as songwriters, as co-producers, as artists than I think anyone really ever realized," says Ebbin. "When we started that [first] record they learned a lot. They've worked with a lot of great producers, and they've worked with a lot of great songwriters. These guys are not passive rock stars. These guys work hard and they care about the craft. When I got into a room with those guys, they had a big vocabulary of stuff, a big toolbox of tricks, and I think we ended up with an amalgamation of all that. The fact that they were super open to new ideas just made things flow really easily, and that's the best way to have that creative process."

With their artistic batteries recharged, the Jersey Syndicate would next look back at and reevaluate their catalog, resulting in a reinterpreted greatest hits and opening their vault of unreleased music to the public for the first time. Then it would be time for a new adventure, one that seems obvious in retrospect but which may have surprised some at the time.

DIVING INTO THE VAULTS

A FTER THE BACK-TO-BACK SUCCESS OF TWO NEW STUDIO ALBUMS, JON AND THE BON JOVI CLAN DECIDED TO TAKE A LOOK BACK AT THEIR CATALOG, BOTH IN TERMS OF REINTERPRETING SOME OF THEIR CLASSIC SONGS AS WELL AS PULLING OUT SOME NEVER-BEFORE-HEARD TRACKS.

Released in November 2003 and co-produced by Patrick Leonard (who worked extensively with Madonna throughout the eighties and after), *This Left Feels Right* circumvented the concept of a greatest-hits package by allowing the band to redo their hits in a predominately acoustic format. While the intent was good, many of the reinterpretations seem a bit forced. There were some interesting alternative ideas: the harp and piano on "It's My Life," the strings and sultry vocals of their producer's then-wife Olivia D'Abo on "Livin' on a Prayer," turning "You Give Love a Bad Name" into a bluesy torch song, not to mention the country tinge on some tracks that prefaced the group's Nashville-inspired *Lost Highway* album three years later.

The live concert DVD, *This Left Feels Right Live*, which was directed by Jon's brother Anthony, worked better as it mixed in other originals and covers that were not reworkings, and the ecstatic energy of the crowd added to the atmosphere. The live DVD showcased the first time that Jon had expanded the group into an eight-piece unit, including two members of the Asbury Jukes on loan—guitarist Bobby Bandiera and keyboardist Jeff Kazee. It would not be the last.

A far better release was the 2004 box set *100,000,000 Bon Jovi Fans Can't Be Wrong*, a five-disc collection of B-sides, rare tracks, video clips, and predominantly unreleased songs and demos from throughout the band's then twenty-year recording career. Inspired by Elvis, the cover featured the band members in gold lamé suits, mirroring the cover of Presley's 1959 compilation *50,000,000 Elvis Fans Can't Be Wrong*. While the King's collection was comprised of hit singles and B-sides, the Bon Jovi set encompassed fifty-one tracks, three-quarters of which were unreleased. A few more were European B-sides and movie soundtrack cuts.

The group's superlative *Keep the Faith* was represented by no fewer than twelve cuts, ten of which were unreleased. Those songs proved to this writer that his assertion that it is their best album was correct. Tracks like the anthemic "The Radio Saved My Life Tonight," the swaggering "Sympathy," and the moody "Satellite" could have easily made *Faith*'s final cut.

The set also offered insight into the various stages of the band. The Iron Maiden-ish tune "We Rule the Night," pulled from their second album, shows how they were once toying with a heavier sound. The Johnny Cash-like vibe of "Last Man Standing" foreshadowed their Nashville album and also served as a template for its hard-rocking rendition on their next studio album, *Have a Nice Day*. The Motown style "Love Is a Four Letter Word" served up that R&B flavor that Sambora loves to have coming through. "Rich Man in a Poor Man's House"—a *Crush* outtake co-written by Jon and Dave Stewart—was Bon Jovi by way of Tom Petty. Tico, Richie, and David all had a song showcasing their lead vocals. For Richie, it was an unreleased solo tune; for Tico, a debut album castaway featuring the accordion; and for David, a song from his yet to be seen Broadway musical *Memphis*.

Complete with two essays and written commentary from Jon on every track, *100,000,000 Bon Jovi Fans Can't Be Wrong* is the kind of box set more bands should release for devout fans. Of course, that is what Bon Jovi claimed they were about from the start.

ABOVE AND RIGHT: Japanese ads for the *This Left Feels Right* collection of reinterpreted Bon Jovi classics.

X

MAKING MEMORIES

2004—2008

TRUE TO FORM, FOR THEIR NEXT ALBUM BON JOVI DECIDED TO TRY OUT A NEW PRODUCER, AND THIS TIME IT WOULD BE JOHN SHANKS, ANOTHER STUDIO SCULPTOR WITH A POP PEDIGREE—AT THE TIME HE HAD WORKED WITH HIT ARTISTS LIKE MELISSA ETHERIDGE, STEVIE NICKS, MICHELLE BRANCH, HILARY DUFF, AND SHERYL CROW. WHILE BON JOVI WERE ASSEMBLING THEIR EXTENSIVE BOX SET, THEY BEGAN TO WORK ON THEIR NINTH ALBUM IN SUMMER 2004 AND SHANKS DECIDED THAT THEIR USUAL APPROACH SHOULD BE JETTISONED.

Jon and Richie were used to writing and doing a lot of demos, but Shanks encouraged them to write in the studio and use a drum machine, then bring Tico and Hugh in at the end of the process to add in their parts. In press materials for the album, Jon said the group's rhythm section played on the album for a day and a half in total. Their producer strived for immediacy in the music.

The group had expected to release *Have a Nice Day* that fall, but Jon felt that the songs were not quite there yet. In the interim, Bon Jovi received the Award for Merit at the American Music Awards in November. (Jon's third son Romeo Jon Bongiovi had entered the world on March 29, 2004. Tico's son Hector Alexander arrived earlier, on January 9, 2004. Richie received an honorary doctorate in humanities from Kean University in May 2004.) More songwriting continued, but by the time Jon and Richie had more material, Shanks was unavailable to continue, so they enlisted producer Rick Parashar, who had worked with Nickelback and 3 Doors Down. He helped them complete the album with four album cuts ("Story of My Life," "Novocaine," "Last Cigarette," and "Wildflower") and a single B-side ("Dirty Little Secret"), most of which were catchy numbers that injected the album with more hard rock energy. Co-written by David Bryan, "Last Cigarette" was akin to a more adult version of "Bad Medicine" in its tale of an alluring but toxic love connection, this time with a slight sense of anxiety.

The title track and first single certainly had a snarky edge to it, while "Last Man Standing"—a rocked-up version of the Johnny Cash-style tune from *This Left Feels Right*

PAGE 154: Tico behind his kit, emblazoned with the famous heart-and-dagger logo, on May 16, 2005, in New York.

OPPOSITE: Left to right: David, Tico, Jon, and Richie show off their Award of Merit from the American Music Awards in November 2004, at the Shrine Auditorium in Los Angeles.

Live and the box set—amplified the desperation of a musician coping with digital trickery encroaching upon the live music experience. The edgier side of the album was indicative of the mindset that Jon was in at the time, and no doubt he was disappointed by the re-election of George W. Bush as president of the United States, especially given that he stumped for Democratic candidate John Kerry the year before (as he had done for Al Gore in 2000). In a television interview with Yahoo! Music Japan in 2005, Jon said that despite the cynicism inherent in the title track, he wanted the album to offer a sense of inclusion after the polarizing election cycle.

Fans responded favorably to the solid new collection as the album rocketed to Number 2 upon its debut. The video for "Have a Nice Day" featured the band exploring New York while the sarcastic smiley face image from the album cover was spread around via flyers, plastered on construction sites, even sculpted out of crops in a field. It was the organic equivalent to a viral internet meme, perhaps echoing the sentiment of "Last Man Standing" and the appeal of natural versus digital art.

Yet despite that classic Bon Jovi anthem making waves, another song would prove to be the breakout hit of the album: "Who Says You Can't Go Home." Originally done up as a folksy tune, the band had a second version recorded with Jennifer Nettles trading off with Jon on vocals and some twangy guitar added in, both courtesy of major country producer Dann Huff (who, funnily enough, was in the hard rock band Giant at the dawn of the nineties). Jon originally collaborated with Keith Urban on the track but he found their voices to be too similar. When Jennifer Nettles was brought in later, she had the vocal sound that Jon was seeking. She may have been unknown to rock fans, but her country band Sugarland's debut album *Twice the Speed of Life* was a platinum hit in the States and would reach double platinum by the following January.

Even before their new album came out, Bon Jovi played with Sugarland on an episode of *CMT Crossroads* that was recorded in August 2005 and broadcast in September, two months before *Have a Nice Day* was released. At the start of the tour in mid-November, Bon Jovi appeared with Nettles to perform the song on the CMA Awards, and they would repeat that performance at the Daytona 500 in February 2006. When "Who Says You Can't Go Home" was officially released in March 2006, it rose to Number 23 on the Top 100. Even more

ABOVE: The members of Bon Jovi receiving plaques for platinum sales of *Have a Nice Day* in Germany at a press conference in Dusseldorf on May 13, 2006. Hugh McDonald (far left) makes a rare public photo appearance.

OPPOSITE: Poster-style ticket for one of Bon Jovi's stops on their British leg of the *Have a Nice Day* stadium tour.

HAVE A NICE DAY ALBUM

Release date: September 20, 2005
Recording studios: Sanctuary Sound II, New Jersey; Ocean Way
Recording, Hollywood, California.
Producers: John Shanks, Jon Bon Jovi, Richie Sambora, Rick
Parashar, Dann Huff, Desmond Child (exec.)
Singles: "Have a Nice Day," "Who Says You Can't Go Home,"
"Welcome to Wherever You Are," "I Want to Be Loved"
Top chart positions: 2 (US, *Billboard*), 2 (UK)

1. "Have a Nice Day" (Bon Jovi, Sambora, Shanks; 3:48)
2. "I Want to Be Loved" (Bon Jovi, Sambora, Shanks; 3:49)
3. "Welcome to Wherever You Are" (Bon Jovi, Sambora, Shanks; 3:47)
4. "Who Says You Can't Go Home" (Bon Jovi, Sambora; 4:40)
5. "Last Man Standing" (Bon Jovi, Billy Falcon; 4:37)
6. "Bells of Freedom" (Bon Jovi, Sambora, Child; 4:55)
7. "Wildflower" (Bon Jovi; 4:13)
8. "Last Cigarette" (Bon Jovi, David Bryan; 3:38)
9. "I Am" (Bon Jovi, Sambora, Shanks; 3:53)
10. "Complicated" (Bon Jovi, Falcon, Max Martin; 3:37)
11. "Novocaine" (Bon Jovi; 4:49)
12. "Story of My Life" (Bon Jovi, Falcon; 4:08)
13. "Who Says You Can't Go Home" (duet version with Jennifer
    Nettles) (Bon Jovi, Sambora; 3:50)

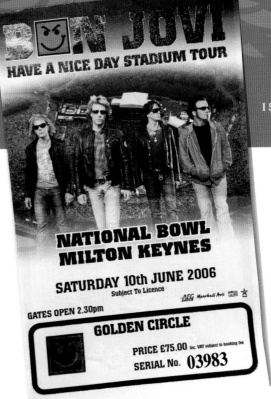

impressive, Bon Jovi became the first rock band to
score a Number 1 hit on *Billboard*'s Hot Country
Songs chart. In 2007, the song finally secured the
group's first Grammy Award win in the Best Country
Collaboration with Vocals category. The seeds for
their Nashville album had been sowed.

Another pre-album preview occurred on
September 21, 2005, when the band appeared
on *The Oprah Winfrey Show* for the first time,
performing "It's My Life" and "You Give Love a Bad
Name." Jon chatted with Oprah about his life and
career between songs. The energy from the almost
entirely female crowd was ebullient. Women of all
ages from twenties to fifties were screaming their
approval. It was like Beatlemania again, but this time on home turf. The appearance was
significant because, beyond allying themselves with one of television's biggest stars, the
band was acknowledging the fact that despite gaining new fans recently, their core audience
was growing older and they were growing with them. The group was aging nicely, particularly
heartthrobs Jon and Richie, and the Oprah alliance spawned future appearances from Jon
and the band through her various media channels and like-minded daytime talk shows
including *Ellen*.

Commencing in November, the *Have a Nice Day* tour was a major success across the
globe: eighty-nine shows spanning three continents that grossed $131 million, making it
the third-highest-grossing tour in the world for 2006 according to *Billboard* magazine.
Three of the last six shows in late July 2006 took place at Giants Stadium. That sold-out
trio grossed $11.3 million.

OF ALL THE BON JOVI CONCERTS I'VE SEEN OVER THE YEARS, THE CHRISTMAS SHOWS AT THE COUNT BASIE THEATRE ARE THE MOST MEMORABLE. NOT ONLY BECAUSE IT WAS A TREAT TO SEE THEM IN A SMALL VENUE, BUT I THINK THE BAND WENT OUT OF THEIR WAY TO MAKE THEM SPECIAL FOR THE FANS. THEY WOULD PLAY LOTS OF COOL COVER SONGS AND EVERY MEMBER GOT THEIR OWN CHANCE TO SING LEAD. DURING THE ONE IN 1995, DAVID SANG 'TUMBLING DICE' FROM THE ROLLING STONES, TICO SANG A WILLIE NELSON SONG CALLED 'CRAZY,' AND RICHIE DID AN AMAZING JOB ON STEVIE WONDER'S 'HEAVEN HELP US.' THEY TRULY SEEMED TO BE ENJOYING THEMSELVES, AND YOU GOT TO SEE WHAT A TIGHT BAND THEY REALLY WERE.

Gail Flug, veteran music journalist, January 2016

OPPOSITE, TOP LEFT: Richie Sambora clearly knows the way to San Jose as Bon Jovi played at the HP Pavilion there on February 27, 2006.

OPPOSITE, TOP RIGHT: Jon Bon Jovi embraces the drama of the arena during the *Have a Nice Day* world tour on June 13, 2006, at Kingston Communications Stadium in Hull, United Kingdom.

OPPOSITE, BOTTOM: Sugarland singer Jennifer Nettles joins Jon Bon Jovi onstage to duet with him during their hit country rendition of "Who Says You Can't Go Home" at the Philips Arena in Atlanta, Georgia, on January 17, 2006.

RIGHT: This ticket displays the famed Bon Jovi heart-and-dagger "logo."

Multiplatinum Canadian hard-rockers Nickelback supported Bon Jovi on their European and North American tour dates between May and July 2006. Nickelback bassist Mike Kroeger tells me that the members and crew of Bon Jovi treated them really well and respectfully. "As the tour went on, we started hanging out more and more with them and going places with them on days off," he tells me. "At one point, Jon had his family come out when we were in Ireland, and it was cool to see the guy who's singing 'You Give Love a Bad Name' with his wife and kids and having to be a dad. I loved it because I'm a dad and I take that very seriously, and I saw that he did, too."

Mike felt that there was a connection between the two groups and their followers. "The reason why we were really interested in touring with those guys is that we felt like their fans could be our fans too, but they just didn't know it yet," the bassist says. "The attitude we took into this was if these people like Bon Jovi, they're probably going to like us, so let's just show them what we do and we can share fans with them. And that's really what happened. The Bon Jovi contingent of fans very much adopted us, and we can thank Bon Jovi for that."

He adds that there was a group of British ladies who he first saw on the Bon Jovi tour who had seen the Jersey rockers on every tour since around 1987. "Now they come to our shows and get right out front where we can see and hold up a sign that says how many times they've seen Nickelback, which is now thirty or forty," says Kroeger. "It's really cool. Touring with Bon Jovi basically helped us open Europe. We can hold them responsible for that [because] they gave us a chance."

LOST HIGHWAY ALBUM

Release date: June 19, 2007
Recording studios: Black Bird Studios, Nashville; NGR Recording, Hollywood
Producers: John Shanks, Dann Huff, Desmond Child (exec.)
Singles: "(You Want to) Make a Memory," "Lost Highway," "Till We Ain't Strangers Anymore," "Whole Lotta Leavin'"
Top chart positions: 1 (US *Billboard*), 2 (UK)

1. "Lost Highway" (Jon Bon Jovi, Richie Sambora, Shanks; 4:13)
2. "Summertime" (Bon Jovi, Sambora, Shanks; 3:17)
3. "(You Want to) Make a Memory" (Child, Bon Jovi, Sambora; 4:36)
4. "Whole Lotta Leavin'" (Bon Jovi, Shanks; 4:16)
5. "We Got It Going On" (featuring Big & Rich) (Bon Jovi, Sambora, Kenny Alphin, John Rich; 4:13)
6. "Any Other Day" (Bon Jovi, Sambora, Gordie Sampson; 4:01)
7. "Seat next to You" (Bon Jovi, Sambora, Hillary Lindsey; 4:21)
8. "Everybody's Broken" (Bon Jovi, Billy Falcon; 4:11)
9. "Till We Ain't Strangers Anymore" (featuring LeAnn Rimes) (Bon Jovi, Sambora, Brett James; 4:43)
10. "The Last Night" (Bon Jovi, Sambora, Shanks; 3:32)
11. "One Step Closer" (Bon Jovi, Sambora, Shanks; 3:35)
12. "I Love This Town" (Bon Jovi, Sambora, Falcon; 4:36)

When Bon Jovi began work on their tenth album the next year, they knew it was going to be a different kind of effort. Buoyed by the success of "Who Says You Can't Go Home," they sought to do a Nashville-inspired album. It seemed like a natural choice given the country slant to a few of their songs over the years, but the head of their label, Lucian Grainge (CEO of Universal) was skeptical, so they agreed that Bon Jovi would deliver a greatest-hits album in exchange for a seemingly risky venture.

The group enlisted producers Dann Huff and John Shanks, country stars LeAnn Rimes and Big & Rich, songwriters Desmond Child, Billy Falcon, and Darrell Brown, and country singer-songwriters Gordie Sampson, Hillary Lindsey, and Brett James to collaborate on an album that would pay homage to their Nashville influences without attempting to do a flat-out country album. The approach made sense. Many rock and pop acts had been slowly veering toward country for a few years, while many country pop artists were writing songs that echoed the pop-rock of the 1980s—the decadent decade in which Bon Jovi became superstars. The trick was not to co-opt the country image or style but remain respectful to the influence.

"It's a very ballsy move to try something different," Dann Huff told journalist Deborah Evans Price of the CMA Close Up News Service on October 10, 2007. "It's reinventing at a point when you really don't need to reinvent. That takes a lot of courage and integrity. But you can't draw a boundary around the way people are going to tell stories about their lives and loves and the things they write about. I can't tell you that 'Make a Memory' [the first single from *Lost Highway*] is a country song. I can't tell you it's a pop song. But I do think it's an emotional song that people are digging. It's just about music that touches people. So I hope the lines get blurred."

The *Lost Highway* album purposefully straddled the line between the rock and country worlds. The title track ("One Step Closer"), "Everybody's Broken," and "A Whole Lotta

ABOVE: Backstage pass for a behind-the-scenes experience with Jon Bon Jovi from one of his solo shows.

OPPOSITE: Bon Jovi's master of keyboards David Bryan strikes a dramatic pose during the New York City stop on the *Lost Highway* tour on July 14, 2008.

LORENZA PONCE:
STRING SIDEKICK

AFREQUENT PRESENCE ON STAGE WITH BON JOVI AND JON AS A SOLO ARTIST OVER THE LAST DECADE HAS BEEN VIOLINIST EXTRAORDINAIRE LORENZA PONCE, WHO BRINGS A LIVELY FLAIR TO THEIR SHOWS.

A classically trained player, she began to gain recognition while performing as a featured player in Kitaro's *An Enchanted Evening* in 1995 and John Tesh's *One World* concert in 1999, both of which aired on PBS. She has also toured with those new age icons, and since that time has worked with a wide range of artists, including Sheryl Crow, Hall and Oates (as lead violinist and string contractor), and the Dixie Chicks (as string contractor/arranger for their Top of the World tour).

Lorenza joined the Bon Jovi family when she was enlisted for the *Tribute to Heroes* telethon and the Concert for New York, after which she became a permanent member of Jon's solo band, the Kings of Suburbia, and was the violinist and backing vocalist on the *Lost Highway* trek. Lorenza has certainly had some great travel adventures on her global treks with Bon Jovi, from Europe to Asia to Australia. In a 2010 interview with crime thriller author Cat Connor, she talked about taking a picture of herself in the Indian Ocean and making a stop-off in Tasmania. But the highlight for her was when they went Down Under.

"Once we got to New Zealand we had only one day there," Ponce told Connor on November 19, 2010. "I'm a huge *Lord of the Rings* fan. Christchurch, New Zealand, is where a lot of the *Lord of the Rings* scenes from the movies were shot. Jon thought it was so funny that I am such a huge fan of the movies that he actually let me miss sound check to take a day-long tour of the movie locations. Normally, the only allowable excuse to miss sound check is death."

While most of Lorenza's solo albums have had a new age/contemporary slant to them, rock 'n' roll took a hold of her soul so that on her 2010 album *Soul Shifter* she explored a roots-rock sound that she found refreshing. In a 2011 interview with Chris M. Junior of Medleyville.us, Lorenza discussed adapting her playing to rock for that album. "Because the violin has no frets, it is very conducive to sliding," she said. "Some of the greatest guitar solos are done on slide guitar, so I have studied that aspect of playing. I've incorporated that into my soloing—I sound like Nigel from *Spinal Tap* [*laughs*]—because a violin does that so nicely. It actually sounds really cool if you throw a delay on it; then it has a lot more expression and it definitely sets it apart from the classical violin or a fiddler."

Lorenza has hung out with some major cultural icons—she has had tea with Mick Jagger, met Muhammad Ali, and performed at the Commander in Chief Ball during President Obama's inauguration—and she still loves classical. At the end of 2015, she joined the string quartet Quartetto Tomassini, which performs Latin, jazz, American standards, and classical pieces. It is this versatility that has made her a valuable asset to everyone from Adele to Bon Jovi.

ABOVE: Richie Sambora, Lorenza Ponce, and Jon Bon Jovi rocking the Ricoh Arena in Coventry, United Kingdom, on June 24, 2008.

▲▲ BEING ASKED TO BE THE SOLO VIOLINIST ON THE BON JOVI *LOST HIGHWAY* TOUR, THE BIGGEST TOUR OF 2008, AND A FEMALE, NO LESS. THAT WAS A REALLY BIG DEAL, TO BE LET INTO THE BOYS' CLUB FOR A TOUR. I MET SARAH FERGUSON, DUCHESS OF YORK, AT A SHOW, AND SHE TOLD ME HOW 'BRILLIANT' SHE THOUGHT IT WAS THAT BON JOVI HAD DECIDED TO HAVE A WOMAN ONSTAGE! ▼▼

Lorenza Ponce to Hal B. Selzer, *Aquarian Weekly*, May 26, 2010

Leavin' Going On" (inspired by Richie and David's recent painful divorces) all fitted comfortably within the country crossover realm, whereas the pounding "Summertime" and "I Love This Town" were rowdy arena anthems. Modest hit ballads like "(You Want to) Make a Memory" and "Till We Ain't Strangers Anymore" (with LeAnn Rimes) sat nicely in the middle. The latter song produced a romantic video starring Jon and LeAnn. Bon Jovi also promoted "Memory" with *American Idol* appearances on May 1 and 2, 2007. Around then the band covered Leonard Cohen's "Hallelujah" as an overseas bonus track, and the acclaimed version was performed on the tour.

Duplicating the success of *Have a Nice Day*, *Lost Highway* became the band's first Number 1 debut and third Number 1 album overall, topping the charts in eight other countries and becoming another platinum-selling album in the United States, with at least a million more units sold overseas. In an era of dwindling album sales, those were more than respectable figures. And the initial limited number of ten concert dates soon blossomed into a nine-month, ninety-nine show tour that crossed five continents and grossed $210 million. Pollstar ranked it as the fifth-highest-grossing tour in North America that year. *Billboard* marked it as the Number 1 tour in the world in 2008.

Beyond the monetary gains, this tour was notable for being the first time that Jon had expanded the group to include other players on tour: in this case, violinist Lorenza Ponce, pedal steel guitar player Kurt Johnson, and Asbury Jukes guitarist Bobby Bandiera. Much like

ABOVE AND OPPOSITE TOP: Richie and Jon show solidarity (above) and the band puts on a dazzling display (opposite) at the Ricoh Arena in Coventry, United Kingdom. The group's newer Nashville-inspired sound resonated with international audiences.

OPPOSITE BOTTOM: Ticket to Bon Jovi's gig at Croke Park, Dublin, on May 20, 2006.

MAKING MEMORIES

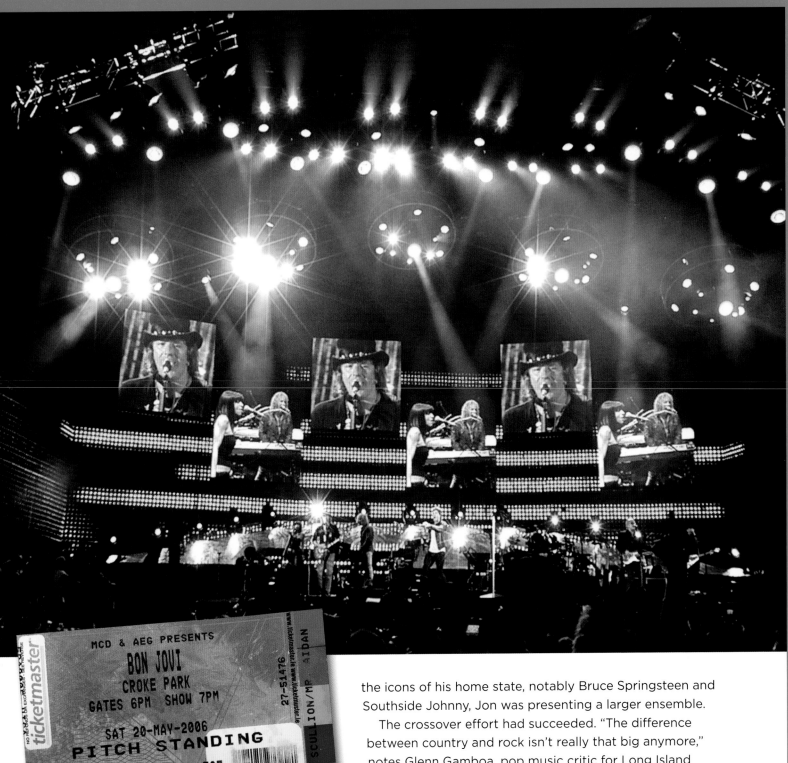

the icons of his home state, notably Bruce Springsteen and Southside Johnny, Jon was presenting a larger ensemble.

The crossover effort had succeeded. "The difference between country and rock isn't really that big anymore," notes Glenn Gamboa, pop music critic for Long Island newspaper *Newsday*, when we speak. "And Bon Jovi's a smart guy, he recognizes that. He saw that he could add a whole bunch of new fans to his fanbase without changing all that much, so that's what he did. The show had a lot more new music than it usually does, but the styles and the presentation weren't that different. It was a Bon Jovi show."

Another significant event happened on the *Lost Highway* tour. The group allowed filmmaker Phil Griffin, who had previously directed a Britney Spears documentary and a Donny Osmond concert video, to follow them on tour to assemble a black-and-white documentary about their lives on and off stage. Intimate interviews were also conducted to let fans glean more about their individual mindsets. Entitled *Bon Jovi: When We Were Beautiful*, the film would debut in 2009 at the Tribeca Film Festival.

The group had conquered the world again and even found yet another audience to cross over to. Their concerts were massive. They had new hits to play and were not just performing a nostalgic set. Life was good. But there was something that they needed to do.

It was time to rock again.

PHILANTHROPIC PURSUITS

J ON BON JOVI HAS BECOME A MAJOR PHILANTHROPIC FIGURE OVER THE LAST FEW YEARS, BOTH SPEARHEADING HIS OWN ORGANIZATION AND CONTRIBUTING TO OTHERS.

The Jon Bon Jovi (JBJ) Soul Foundation has its roots in the Philadelphia Soul—a franchise team in the Arena Football League (AFL) that was started in 2004 through the investments of Jon and Craig Spencer along with minority owners Richie Sambora, former Philadelphia Eagles quarterback Ron Jaworski, and Leo Carlin Jr. Two years on, the Philadelphia Soul Charitable Foundation was started to address issues of hunger and homelessness, with Mimi Box brought onboard as its executive director. She had previously worked with the Philadelphia Eagles for eighteen years, which was how she met Jon. When the AFL temporarily folded before the 2009 season, Jon and his investors pulled out of the team, and he renamed the organization the Jon Bon Jovi Soul Foundation.

Since then, the JBJ Soul Foundation, which was spawned from a discussion Jon had with his wife, Dorothea, has worked to rebuild and refurbish homes through organizations such as Project H.O.M.E., Habitat for Humanity, and Rebuilding Together. They have also worked to build homeless shelters and a safe house for victims of domestic violence. The JBJ Soul Kitchen, for which Dorothea is the program manager for the kitchen program, is an unusual enterprise that has two locations, one in Red Bank and a new center in Tom's River. Unlike soup kitchens, these are full-service restaurants that only require $10 vouchers per person or family. If someone cannot afford that fee, they can volunteer in the kitchen to earn their meal. The JBJ Soul Foundation continues to ally itself with organizations that take care of the homeless and hungry.

Since 1990, the members of Bon Jovi have held an annual concert event every December at the Count Basie Theatre to raise money for places such as local food banks and women's shelters. They charge premium ticket prices to ensure that the maximum funds can be raised (and fans get a fun, off-the-cuff show in an intimate space).

It is actually refreshing when rockers get older and try to do something to change things. There are the stereotypes of the hedonistic rock stars (and there is room for those, too), but that is not an iconography that Jon ever embraced. It is becoming more common to see him wearing a suit and tie these days, even for solo gigs.

"My whole genre, my whole decade of music, I didn't want to be them when I was a kid," Bon Jovi told *USA Today*'s Nancy Dunham on May 29, 2014. "Some journalists tell me, 'You're not very rock 'n' roll.' If all they think is that I should throw a TV out the window, then I'm not interested in talking to them. I don't live the cliché, rock star life."

The other members of Bon Jovi have also been involved with causes that are dear to their hearts. Richie has been engaged with numerous organizations over the years, including the Midnight Mission (a Los Angeles-based homeless charity), City Hearts: Kids Say Yes to the Arts (arts education for at-risk youth in Southern California), MusiCares, Precious Paws, and Memorial Sloan-Kettering (the cancer center that cared for his father before he passed away).

David has been a big advocate for VH1's Save the Music Program, which promotes improving and restoring music education in schools around the country, Only Make Believe, which introduces children with chronic illnesses and disabilities to the joyful world of theater, and he has also lent some sweat and muscle to Habitat for Humanity.

Tico founded the Tico Torres Children's Foundation to help kids find relief from hunger, disease, homelessness, neglect, abuse, and illness. One way he raises money for various child-based organizations is through his annual Tico Torres Celebrity Golf Classic.

OPPOSITE: Jon appears at a Habitat for Humanity event in Detroit, Michigan, on July 7, 2008. His Philadelphia Soul Charitable Foundation joined forces with Habitat for Humanity Detroit and other organizations to help five Detroit families obtain home ownership. The two different videos for "Who Says You Can't Go Home" promoted Jon's work with Habitat for Humanity. Jon has also teamed up with fashion designer Kenneth Cole over the years to raise money for charity.

XI

BACK TO ROCK, STILL ON TOP

2009—2012

THERE IS A POINT AT WHICH ICONIC BANDS WHO HAVE OUTLASTED TRENDS AND DIFFICULT PERIODS START REAPING ACCOLADES AND THE BENEFITS OF THEIR HARD WORK. 2009 CERTAINLY BECAME AN IMPORTANT YEAR FOR BON JOVI IN THAT REGARD. IN APRIL, A FEW MONTHS INTO WORKING ON THEIR ELEVENTH ALBUM *THE CIRCLE*, PHIL GRIFFIN'S DOCUMENTARY *BON JOVI: WHEN WE WERE BEAUTIFUL* DEBUTED AT THE TRIBECA FILM FESTIVAL IN NEW YORK CITY. THE EIGHTY-MINUTE BLACK-AND-WHITE FILM MADE FOR A STARK CONTRAST TO THE STRIKINGLY COLORFUL EIGHTIES BAND THAT MANY PEOPLE REMEMBER, BUT WHICH HAD NOW TRANSFORMED INTO A MORE MATURE ROCK OUTFIT.

The film was revelatory on many fronts. Richie and Tico admitted their varying battles with alcohol and personal demons. David confessed that while it bothered him a bit that Jon was always steering the ship, their success was proof that he was doing something right. The singer himself came off as a driven taskmaster who is gracious with his fans and supportive of his band, but someone who could be very tough to work for.

"I sided with that when I saw that because that's what makes him so great," counters entertainment reporter Cheryl Hoahing. "He is a perfectionist. He wants everything to be done right and done well. That's why the shows are so great." That kid who used to spar with his old bandmates over driving ahead full bore was still doing so in adulthood. He had not lost that passion and was actively trying to buy an NFL team, a goal that has not come to fruition yet, including unsuccessfully bidding for the Buffalo Bills in 2014.

The group also discussed their outside endeavors: Richie's other music projects, Tico's art, David's Broadway work, and Jon's philanthropy. In the film, Richie discussed how personal growth was important to the band and its members. He also expressed a strong desire to do another solo record, but it would be another three years before that transpired.

PAGE 170: At age forty-eight, Jon is still the youthful rock star performing onstage at the New Meadowlands Stadium in East Rutherford, New Jersey, on May 26, 2010.

ABOVE: Left to right: David Bryan, Tico Torres, Richie Sambora, and Jon Bon Jovi attend the world premiere of the documentary *Bon Jovi: When We Were Beautiful* at the 2009 Tribeca Film Festival in New York City on April 29, 2009.

In June, Jon and Richie were inducted into the Songwriters Hall of Fame at their fortieth annual ceremony. It was a nice accolade for a duo whose work had often been derided by numerous critics. The first person who Jon thanked was his wife Dorothea, which received immediate applause, and he told Chris Daughtry he sang "that song" ("Blaze of Glory," which they performed live when they toured together in 2008) better than he did. "The business is changing on us," Bon Jovi told the attendees. "One thing they can't take away is the song."

A month later on May 3, Jon Bon Jovi was inducted into the New Jersey Hall of Fame by the state's then-governor Jon Corzine. He was praised for his music, his humanitarian work, and for his loyalty to his home state. Governor Corzine described Jon as "a man of character" and "talented, scrappy, self-made, and willing to give back." He accepted the award as the house band performed "Who Says You Can't Go Home." As the band finished up their recording sessions in Los Angeles in June, another magical moment transpired.

Persian singer Andy Madadian is an Iranian-born Armenian exile who left Iran thirty-five years ago, "The Persian Elvis" whose music is banned there because it was deemed "too sexy" for the populace. His homeland was on the verge of a revolution because of hotly contested election results. Andy had known iconic producer and musician Don Was for a long time and they shared mutual admiration and a desire to work together on something special.

That something would become a spontaneous cover intended to send a message of hope and solidarity to the troubled people of Iran. Bon Jovi were finishing up the recording of *The Circle* in John Shanks's studio and Don took Andy down there with the thought of recording Ben E. King's "Stand by Me." As Don told ABC News, Jon, Richie, and John were eating lunch. Don made his pitch, and they went for it.

"Together we did the track in one afternoon," Madadian tells me. "Any musician they called came down and played. The video and audio, everything was in one afternoon. It was just a miracle. I have to give Jon the credit because his mind works like his singing, his thinking, his planning—he organized the whole thing. He's a manager, he's a producer, he's an intellectual, he's a humanitarian. Everything in that track tells you what kind of a person he is."

Andy says that Jon wanted to sing a few lines in Farsi (the entire first verse is sung in the Persian language), so he learned quickly and without hesitation. "How often do you find an American artist say, 'I want to explore that, I want to touch this language'," observes

SONGWRITERS
HALL of FAME

THE CIRCLE ALBUM

Release date: November 10, 2009
Recording studios: Sanctuary Studios, New Jersey, and Henson
Recording Studios, California
Producers: John Shanks, Jon Bon Jovi (co-producer), Richie
Sambora (co-producer)
Singles: "We Weren't Born to Follow," "Superman Tonight,"
"When We Were Beautiful," "Work for the Working Man" (Promo)
Top chart positions: 1 (US, *Billboard*), 2 (UK)

1. "We Weren't Born to Follow" (Bon Jovi, Sambora; 4:03)
2. "When We Were Beautiful" (Bon Jovi, Sambora, Billy Falcon; 5:18)
3. "Work for the Working Man" (Bon Jovi, Sambora, Darrell Brown; 4:04)
4. "Superman Tonight" (Bon Jovi, Sambora, Falcon; 5:12)
5. "Bullet" (Bon Jovi, Sambora; 3:50)
6. "Thorn In My Side" (Bon Jovi, Sambora; 4:05)
7. "Live Before You Die" (Bon Jovi, Sambora; 4:17)
8. "Brokenpromiseland" (Bon Jovi, Sambora, John Shanks, Desmond
   Child; 4:57)
9. "Love's the Only Rule" (Bon Jovi, Sambora, Falcon; 4:38)
10. "Fast Cars" (Bon Jovi, Sambora, Child; 3:16)
11. "Happy Now" (Bon Jovi, Sambora, Child; 4:21)
12. "Learn to Love" (Bon Jovi, Sambora, Child; 4:39)

OPPOSITE: Professor Richie Sambora addresses the audience during the fortieth Annual Songwriters Hall of Fame Ceremony at the New York Marriott Marquis on June 18, 2009. He received an honorary doctorate of letters from Kean University in Union, New Jersey, on May 6, 2004, and later that night joined his old bandmate Bruce Foster for a Shark Frenzy reunion show and CD release party at the Holiday Inn Select in Clinton, New Jersey. Bruce says that Richie has never asked for any profits from their reissues.

Madadian, who adds, "I think he sounds fantastic. There is an American accent, but hey, everybody loves Sophia Loren who speaks English still with an accent." Andy's friend Paksima Zakipour wrote new lyrics in Farsi for the opening verse.

"I can't wait for one day when Iran's situation is more moderate so we can go there and play," says Madadian. "People will go crazy if Bon Jovi goes to Iran. You're talking about eighty million people, 70 percent under thirty years old. They're all Bon Jovi fans. We'll keep our fingers crossed. Iranians love heavy rock."

The cover song was not connected to an organization or promoted in any other way than simply presenting it on various YouTube channels, which is how the artists wanted it. Andy went on CNN (on July 4) and on ABC News with Don Was to discuss the song, and as of May 2016, the clip has collectively been viewed over ten million times.

This musical collaboration is significant because it echoed Jon's growing social consciousness and the more serious and sometimes somber tone of *The Circle*, which was a return to the more hard-rocking sounds they had become known for, tempered with socially conscious lyrics addressing their view of the world. The Iranian situation would influence the lead single "We Weren't Born to Follow." The video for "We Weren't Born to Follow"—a montage of famous people and events—played on Jon's ideas about the global human spirit.

Released in November 2009, *The Circle* was grittier than *Lost Highway* and also more contemplative about real world issues. While not as heavy musically as some expected it would be, it was a very solid rock album. Lead single "We Weren't Born to Follow" dealt with their time-honored theme of hope in the wake of adversity, but with a blunter slant than usual. "When We Were Beautiful" was a gorgeous ballad ruminating on innocence lost. "Brokenpromiseland" painted a sketch of people living beyond their means and trying to regroup. Jon told Alan McGee in a November 2009 Q&A in *The Guardian* that the angsty "Bullet" was about Jennifer Hudson's mother, brother, and nephew being shot and murdered in Chicago and that "Happy Now" was about Obama's election as president of the United States.

Of "When We Were Beautiful," Bon Jovi told journalist Talia Soghomonian in an interview on November 6, 2009: "We couldn't have written that song before this [economic] downturn because the world wasn't feeling like that . . . just fourteen months ago, the American stock market was at 14,000 points; everyone had one of those big mansions; it was Bush's last days in office; even the war was a page twenty-five story in the back section of the paper. So the world changed dramatically last October. And it's documented in the songs."

While some critics and fans may have felt that this newer, more serious Bon Jovi seemed incongruous with the good time rockers of old, *The Circle* still resonated with fans enough to have them make it their second album to debut at Number 1 and their fourth Number 1 album overall. It became their fifth Number 1 album in Japan, tying a Western artist record with Mariah Carey and Simon & Garfunkel.

Before the tour started, Bon Jovi received another honor, being asked, along with U2, to perform at the Brandenburg Gate in Berlin to celebrate the twentieth anniversary of the Berlin Wall coming down on November 5. The group had the entire, purple-drenched plaza as their stage and performed "We Weren't Born to Follow" for the crowd who endured a light drizzle during the event. Further, that song became Major League Baseball's post-season theme for 2009, and it was reportedly used in a *Final Fantasy* video game commercial in Japan.

It should also be noted that in late October, David Bryan and Joe DiPietro's musical *Memphis* finally opened on Broadway after a month of previews and nearly fifteen years in development.

A unique promotional opportunity was afforded Bon Jovi for *The Circle*. On October 14, 2009, the *New York Times* reported that for the next two months, Jon and the band would be seen exclusively on television shows falling under the NBC Universal banner, including *Today*, the *Tonight Show*, *Saturday Night Live*, the *NBC Nightly News with Brian Williams*, and *Inside the Actor's Studio* on the Bravo network. Jon was their "artist in residence." The deal made sense given that Bon Jovi's music was being released by the Universal Music Group, and only a rock band of that stature could commandeer that kind of push.

Bon Jovi's tour in 2010 was a phenomenal success, grossing $201 million, making them Pollstar and *Billboard*'s top touring act for 2010. The global trek included a sold-out twelve-night run at London's O$_2$ arena and three sold-out shows opening the New Meadowlands

ABOVE: Bathed in purple light, Bon Jovi performs in front of the Brandenburg Gate in Berlin, Germany, on November 9, 2009, to celebrate the twentieth anniversary of the fall of the Berlin Wall.

OPPOSITE TOP: A formidable frontline at Bon Jovi's concert at the New Meadowlands Stadium during *The Circle* tour. Their three-night stint officially opened the venue. Left to right: Hugh McDonald, Richie Sambora, Jon Bon Jovi, and Bobby Bandiera.

OPPOSITE BOTTOM: Tico "the Hitman" Torres unleashes a truly effervescent performance while Bon Jovi rocks the Palace of Auburn Hills in Auburn Hills, Michigan, on March 17, 2010.

BROADWAY BOUND

(D)AVID BRYAN'S FILM COMPOSING LED TO A BRIEF FORAY INTO OUTSIDE SONGWRITING IN 1995 WHEN HE PENNED THE TOP 30 HIT "THIS TIME" FOR CURTIS STIGERS, A SONG WHICH THAT SINGER COVERED AT THE INSISTENCE OF INDUSTRY MOGUL CLIVE DAVIS.

In 1998, Bryan got a publishing deal thanks to co-writing Bon Jovi's Top 30 hit "In These Arms," which was a big hit in Canada, Australia, Germany, and several other European countries. But future covers by other artists did not surface, and a series of connections led to the keyboardist becoming involved in musical theater. Eventually he scored the Tony-winning Broadway hit *Memphis*—a show loosely based on the story of Dewey Phillips, a Memphis DJ who was one of the first white DJs to play black music in the 1950s, and his fictitious relationship with R&B singer Felicia Farrell. Their onstage interracial romance flared tempers in the racist South.

The road to *Memphis* was not that smooth. When he received the script from writer and fellow New Jersey native Joe DiPietro in 2001, David played around with the lyrics that had been penned and added music to a rapidly produced demo. Joe quickly enlisted David as composer/co-lyricist, and the duo began work on the show in earnest.

Given that Joe had penned the successful show *I Love You, You're Perfect, Now Change*, which had been running off-Broadway for five years (and would go on for seven more and be staged across the world), and because David was the keyboardist in Bon Jovi, they quickly received $1 million in funding between the Mountain View Center for the Performing Arts (outside San Francisco) and the North Shore Music Theatre (outside Boston). The rollicking musical was initially staged in Seattle and Boston during 2003 and 2004. Following those productions, financial and political issues put the show on the back burner. David went back into Bon Jovi land. Joe created the Elvis Presley jukebox musical *All Shook Up* for Broadway.

David and Joe reunited in 2007 to work on *The Toxic Avenger Musical*. Unlike the more R&B and gospel-infused score to *Memphis*, this B-movie parody required a comedic touch. And who better to tackle a show about a Jersey boy turned unlikely superhero via toxic waste than two natives who get the state's mindset? The mirthful musical was tested out in their home state in the fall of 2008 before debuting off-Broadway in April 2009. Driven by a rock-infused score, the show played for nine months and received three Drama Desk Award nominations and won the Outer Critics Circle Award for Best New Off-Broadway Musical. Other productions were mounted in North America.

Memphis came back to life in early 2008 when Christopher Ashley, newly anointed artistic director of the La Jolla Playhouse in San Diego, sought to produce it. Month-long runs in San Diego (late summer 2008) and Seattle (winter 2009) prefaced its Broadway debut in October 2009. In 2010, it won four Tony Awards: Best Musical, Best Book of a Musical, Best Original Score, and Best Orchestrations. It ran until early 2012, and since then it has toured the United States and has had productions mounted in London, Toyko, and Philadelphia.

David found the experience exhilarating. "*Memphis* has nine musicians and twenty-six actors, and I've told everybody what to play," he explained to me in March 2010. "I sit there and do horn parts for the band, then tell everybody what to sing. When I sit there and close my eyes, I've got thirty-five people making my music. It's insane. A musical is the most

complicated beast. We didn't have dance until [choreographer] Sergio [Trujillo] came along. I had guys flipping upside down while singing."

The Bon Jovi keyboardist certainly impressed his musical compatriots. "With *Memphis*, you couldn't have had a better match for coming up with that kind of music," says keyboardist/composer Larry Fast in our interview. "It was a perfect mating of where David's strengths are as that rock 'n' roll pianist who has all the theatrical forces available to him in the storyline of the play. What a great way to put it together. I'm not sure who else you would pick to do that."

"Dave's got a play on Broadway right now and a play off-Broadway and it's now even in a touring company, which is quite an accomplishment for any playwright," Jon declared to journalist Talia Soghomonian in 2009. "To have two plays—that's like Elton John territory. That's pretty big!"

"It's pretty remarkable that he was able to find a niche to stick himself in and do a great job at it, and that's not easy," producer Luke Ebbin says to me. "No one on Broadway cares if you're in Bon Jovi, so I think that he's done a tremendous job to turn what was probably thought of as a side project into a big deal. I remember me, my wife, Doc McGhee, Richie, and Heather Locklear went up to see a preview early on. I just remember sitting there, and Richie and I were looking at each other going, 'Wow, this is tremendous. Who knew he had it in him?' He did a great job."

David and Joe have been working on their next musical, *Chasing the Song*, for a few years. In March 2010, the keyboardist told me that that show takes place in 1960, right before the Beatles came into public consciousness. "So that small window of time when everything was about the songwriter, before bands wrote their own songs," explained Bryan. "People always say, 'How do you write songs? Do the words come first? Does the music come first?' This is going to be about songwriters and have a story as well, and we're still developing it. *Chasing the Song* is [about how] you're always chasing the number one hit as a songwriter." David knows a little bit about being number one.

Stadium in East Rutherford, New Jersey. During the year, the group received the Global Icon Award at the 2010 MTV Europe Music Awards. They played "Superman Tonight" on *American Idol* and "We Weren't Born to Follow" on the British *X-Factor*.

Although Jon was deeply entrenched in the new, he did have the band pull out songs from their first three albums that they had hardly played since the late 1980s and early '90s, including "Roulette," "Come Back," "Get Ready," "Toyko Road," "Blood on Blood," "Living in Sin," and "Let It Rock," which allowed David's organ to envelop arena crowds again. The old school additions, varying in number per show, pleasantly surprised many longtime fans. A standout was when Richie took over lead vocals for "Lay Your Hands on Me" (with a stained glass window video backdrop) and for "Homebound Train," during which David, guitarist Bobby Bandiera, and Richie took turns soloing. It was a welcome change to see David shine like that again.

One clever inclusion in the set was a montage of fans singing along to "Livin' on a Prayer" that was featured on the massive, hatch shell-like video screen dominating their stadium show. People had been selected through a contest, with the winners synced up to the music. It was a testament to the power of the song. Fans' reactions are always so strong that Jon has not had to worry about hitting the high notes in "Prayer" for probably two decades. The fans automatically do it for him, and no one seems to care.

Continuing the nod to the old school, Bon Jovi released their *Greatest Hits* CD and DVD collections just before Halloween, fulfilling Jon's promise to his label (even though *Lost Highway* was a hit). The collection included two new songs, "What Do You Got?" and "No Apologies," and the exclusive double disc Target® store edition had two more new tracks—"This Is Love, This Is Life" and "The More Things Change." That same month, the concert film *The Circle Tour Live from Jersey*, the fourth Bon Jovi concert film directed by Jon's brother Anthony, was shown in American movie theaters.

Naturally, all of this activity did not encourage a break. Instead, a few weeks after *The Circle* tour ended in mid-December, the band hit the road in February for sixty-eight more dates to promote their *Greatest Hits*. For other bands, such excessive touring would be

ABOVE: A show of hands while Bon Jovi performs at the Olympic Stadium in Athens, Greece, on July 20, 2011.

OPPOSITE: Autographed tour memento, now a prized possession with Richie's signature for possibly one of the last times he would appear on a Bon Jovi tour.

WHAT ABOUT NOW ALBUM

Release date: March 8, 2013
Producers: John Shanks, Jon Bon Jovi (co-producer), Richie Sambora (co-producer)
Singles: "Because We Can," "What About Now"
Top chart positions: 1 (US, *Billboard*), 2 (UK)

1. "Because We Can" (Bon Jovi, Sambora, Billy Falcon; 4:00)
2. "I'm With You" (Bon Jovi, Shanks; 3:44)
3. "What About Now" (Bon Jovi, Shanks; 3:45)
4. "Pictures of You" (Bon Jovi, Sambora, Shanks; 3:58)
5. "Amen" (Bon Jovi, Falcon; 4:13)
6. "That's What the Water Made Me" (Bon Jovi, Falcon; 4:26)
7. "What's Left of Me" (Bon Jovi, Sambora, Falcon; 4:35)
8. "Army of One" (Bon Jovi, Sambora, Desmond Child; 4:35)
9. "Thick as Thieves" (Bon Jovi, Sambora, Shanks; 4:58)
10. "Beautiful World" (Bon Jovi, Falcon; 3:49)
11. "Room at the End of the World" (Bon Jovi, Shanks; 5:03)
12. "The Fighter" (Bon Jovi; 4:37)

❝ I THINK IT REALLY ENCAPSULATES THE HUMAN SPIRIT AND UNDERLINES OUR BIGGEST BELIEFS IN OPTIMISM AND ALSO HELPS THOSE WHO WANT AND NEED THEIR ONE VOICE TO BE HEARD. WHEN WE SAW THE IRANIAN UPRISING, THE PROTEST AT THE BEGINNING OF THIS SUMMER, AND THAT GIRL NEDA WHO WAS THE FACE OF THE PROTESTORS, THAT'S THE KIND OF SONG THAT THAT PERSON SHOULD KNOW WAS ABOUT THEM. IT WAS ABOUT THE ANONYMOUS GUY IN TIANANMEN SQUARE. . . . HE/SHE, CHINESE, JAPANESE, GERMAN, FRENCH, L.A. CHICK—THAT'S WHAT THIS SONG IS. ❞

Jon Bon Jovi to journalist Talia Soghomonian, November 6, 2009

> **"I HAD THE GOOD FORTUNE TO WORK WITH JON ON THE *STAND UP GUYS* SOUNDTRACK OF WHICH I WAS COMPOSER. AMONG THE MANY POSITIVE ATTRIBUTES THAT IMPRESSED ME ABOUT HIM, I WAS PARTICULARLY TAKEN BY HIS DRIVE AND FOCUS. HE WAS HIGHLY MOTIVATED AND IT WAS CLEAR HOW THOSE COMBINED TRAITS WOULD BRING HIM SO MUCH SUCCESS. EVEN THOUGH JON HAD ACHIEVED SO MUCH OVER THE DECADES, HE STILL MAINTAINED THE ENERGY AND ENTHUSIASM OF SOMEONE WHO HAD JUST SCORED THEIR FIRST RECORD DEAL. HE WAS A TRUE GENTLEMAN, KIND, CHARMINGLY SELF-EFFACING, RESPECTFUL TO EVERYONE, AND NOTHING BUT A COMPLETE PLEASURE TO BE AROUND."**

Lyle Workman, film composer, January 2016

overkill. Not for Bon Jovi. They kept packing them in. While the band was not indulging in sixteen-month world tours anymore, their shows were possibly longer than ever, often clocking in between two and three hours. By late April, Richie left for a month to check himself into rehab (which he also had done back in 2007). Phil X, who been playing rhythm guitar alongside Bobby Bandiera on the tour, stepped into handle lead chores. This situation would be a foreshadowing of what was to come.

Following the close of the tour, the band then took that much-needed break. It had been an intense couple of years. David got a great boost in June when his musical *Memphis* won four Tony Awards, two of which (Best Original Score and Best Orchestrations) were directly related to his work on the show. Not bad for a rocker from Jersey. Two months later in August, he remarried, this time to Lexi Quaas.

2012 would turn out to be a year of outside projects for the members of Bon Jovi. Jon contributed two songs to the film *Stand Up Guys*, starring Al Pacino, Christopher Walken, and Alan Arkin. One of those tracks, "Not Running Anymore," would surface on the deluxe edition of Bon Jovi's next album, and was nominated for a Golden Globe for Best Original Song—Motion Picture. Richie released his third solo album *Aftermath of the Lowdown* and embarked on a world tour. David Bryan and Joe DiPietro continued developing their third musical, *Chasing the Song*. Tico competed in numerous golf tournaments and continued his work with children's causes as well as Rock Star Baby, the company he founded in 2001, which sells kids' clothing and accessories. By the time the boys in the band reconvened to start their next album, *What About Now*, they had had a chance to recharge their batteries.

"With this record, Jon really wanted to take his time writing, so we took eight months on and off to write the album," producer John Shanks told Paul Tingen of *Sound on Sound* in June 2013. "The entire making, including recording, took about a year, starting in October 2011. We wrote and recorded in many places, including my home studio and Henson Studio C [both are in Los Angeles], Jon's apartment in New York and his studio in New Jersey, and Electric Ladyland and Germano Studios in New York. The songs Jon and I, sometimes with

ABOVE: Jon and David enthrall the masses at Rock in Rio 2013 in Brazil on September 20, 2013, headlining the fifth concert day. The massive festival reportedly drew approximately 600,000 attendees.

Richie, wrote for the album were often written at Jon's apartment or at my home studio, with one or two guitars and a piano, a legal pad, and us recording things into a cassette player or an iPhone®." (After all these years, Jon and Richie still loved cassette players.) "We'd sit together and really hone the lyrics as well as the music. We really aimed for the songs to have depth, and I really like the vulnerability and realism in the lyrics."

In keeping with the big sound the group achieved in the late 1980s, Shanks multitracked the various vocal and instrument parts. The song "Because We Can" had no fewer than forty tracks of drums. But the big sound served to accentuate the big themes of the album, which were certainly presented visually in the very colorful illustrations adorning the CD package: a boxer's hand being wrapped in bandages, a soldier armed with a guitar, the band's heart-and-dagger logo adorned with roses and altered so that the dagger became a knuckle knife, rosary beads hanging from a rearview mirror, and two hot babes in bikinis.

The most straight-ahead, pop-sounding album that Bon Jovi has ever done, which is a mixed bag given the talent in the band, *What About Now* addressed many issues that were on their minds without attempting to be overly political. "This was a snapshot," Bon Jovi told *The Republic*'s Ed Masley on April 24, 2013, invoking topics like the consolidation of corporate America and the bursting of the housing bubble and calling people to action when they are dissatisfied with elected officials.

They took those messages to the masses throughout most of 2013. Once again, the band looked to be unstoppable. *What About Now* became their third straight Number 1 debut and fifth Number 1 album overall. It hit Number 1 or Number 2 in twelve more countries. Tour dates were selling out. Crowds were elated. The band debuted "Because We Can" live on *American Idol*. They were still on top of the world. Their stage show, featuring a bank of video monitors underneath the frame of a massive Cadillac grill and windshield, loomed impressively over everyone. It was their biggest stage show ever.

Then something surprising happened. Halfway through the first North American leg of the tour, Richie quit. Unlike previously it did not seem to be health-oriented; he cited personal issues. Both he and Jon remained silent about what happened. The hiatus might have been fine except for one thing. After a while, it did not look like Richie was coming back.

SOLO SAMBORA

DURING BON JOVI'S BREAK FROM RECORDING AND TOURING IN 2011, RICHIE CHOSE TO DIVE INTO A NEW SOLO ALBUM, HIS FIRST IN FOURTEEN YEARS.

This time around he allied himself with producer Luke Ebbin, who helped bring the band back to life with the *Crush* album in 2000. Luke says he and Richie stayed in touch over the years, contributing a song to a Les Paul tribute record, composing the theme to the gossip show the *Insider*, and supplying their own version of the *Entertainment Tonight* theme song sometime in the mid-2000s.

"We kept it going and would get together and write just for the fun of it," says Ebbin. "Then in 2011, we started writing more, and the stuff was really good. We just kept getting together and writing and writing." Thus they decided to record some tunes, with the producer calling in some musicians he regularly worked with "who I thought would be a great band for Richie, then we put them together and went into the studio. Richie thought let's wing it and not rehearse and see what happens when we're in a room. It was pretty magical. Next thing you know, we had a record."

Co-written with Luke (except for two songs written with Phil Cassens and one with Bernie Taupin), Richie's third solo effort spanned a nice range of styles. "Burn That Candle Down" and "Sugar Daddy" had a big seventies glam sound. "Nowadays" served up straight hard rock. "Every Road Leads Home to You" reflected a strong Coldplay influence. *Aftermath of the Lowdown* had, frankly, the vim and vigor missing from recent Bon Jovi offerings and showed a side of Richie that needed to be heard again. The thoughtful songs spoke of his struggles with addiction, loss, and keeping himself anchored in times of trouble. Friend and longtime songwriting partner Bruce Stephen Foster co-wrote album closer "World," and he says, "Richie and I have written about twenty-five songs together, and we spend a long time writing those words." They spent about eight hours trying to work out a key line in "World."

"We just had a really nice, prolific run, and when that train starts you don't want to stop it," says Ebbin of their creative process on the album. "I thought that was a really cool record. I think we really nailed what he's always wanted to make, pulling all of his influences into these songs, obviously making them his own because that guy's got an incredible vocabulary and musicality."

The intimate connection that Luke felt to Richie and his music continued when they ultimately went on four three- to four-week runs to different parts of the world to promote the album. Luke became the bandleader to get the group rehearsed and up to speed before the tours and each show. When Richie's current girlfriend—talented guitarist Orianthi—joined the band, she and Richie would often share lead work, so Luke became a strong rhythm player to provide balance.

"Every part that four other people can't end up playing, I just ended up playing, key parts on guitar," says Ebbin. "I sang all the backgrounds on the record. It's fun to do two-part harmony with one of the great two-part harmony singers who was the lead singer. It was fun to yell 'Wanted' every night."

Richie and Orianthi have been working on music for a new album that, as of spring 2016, is still in the pipeline.

OPPOSITE: Richie Sambora performs during the Barnstable Brown Kentucky Derby Eve Gala in Louisville, Kentucky, on May 1, 2015. The annual event raises money for the Barnstable Brown Diabetes and Obesity Research Center at the University of Kentucky.

❝ ON THIS RECORD, THERE'S AN AUTHENTICITY AND A VULNERABILITY. AND THERE'S A COMMUNICATIVE ASPECT. I'M TALKING ABOUT ME, BUT THESE SONGS ARE GOING TO BE RELATABLE TO PEOPLE ALL OVER THE PLANET. BECAUSE LIKE I SAID, I'VE HAD THAT BIRD'S EYE VIEW OF THE WORLD OVER THE LAST THIRTY YEARS. I'VE SEEN MUSIC BE THE MOST EVOCATIVE, TRANSFORMATIVE, AND COMMUNICATIVE LANGUAGE IN HUMANITY. I GO TO PLACES WHERE THEY SHOULDN'T EVEN UNDERSTAND OUR LANGUAGE, AND MUSIC BREAKS DOWN THOSE BARRIERS. I'VE BEEN ABLE TO COMMUNICATE TO THE MASSES THROUGH SONGWRITING, AND I'VE BEEN DOING THAT FOR A LONG, LONG TIME. I THINK THIS RECORD WILL DO THAT, TOO. ❞

Richie Sambora to Andrew Leahey, *American Songwriter*, August 24, 2012

XII

A NEW ERA BEGINS

2013—2016

PHIL X SUDDENLY FOUND HIMSELF IN THE DRIVER'S SEAT FOR ONE OF THE PRIME GUITAR SLOTS IN ROCK 'N' ROLL.

With the shock departure of Richie Sambora from Bon Jovi in April 2013, Phil X now had a couple of weeks to learn everything he needed for the next leg of a tour that would stretch out across the world for the rest of the year. As he had done eleven previous shows with the group in 2011, he was up to the task. The thirty-seven-year-old guitarist, whose full name is Philip Eric Xenidis, had already accrued plenty of experience touring and/or recording with different artists, including Triumph, Orianthi, Tommy Lee, Kelly Clarkson, Rob Zombie, and, of course, Jon's old friend Aldo Nova, and he was a music coach for the *Josie and the Pussycats* movie. Now he was the lead guitarist in Bon Jovi.

The Because We Can tour, eventually renamed Because We Did, did not suffer from the loss of Richie. Whether due to massive pre-sales or possibly many fans' hope that he might return from his abrupt hiatus, the world tour was sold out and audiences seemed passionately engaged by the shows. While fan opinion online was divided about the presence of a new lead guitarist, Phil enthusiastically played his heart out—a huge grin plastered on his face during concerts. He told Marty Schwartz from *Guitar Jamz* in 2015 that he got the call while he was shopping in Trader Joe's and was told that he had an hour to get ready for a flight to Calgary, Canada, for a show that night. Phil revisited Bon Jovi songs in transit.

Jon added a crowd-pleasing element into the concerts: inviting a female fan or two (or more) onstage to duet with him during "Who Says You Can't Go Home." The results were meant to be fun rather than harmonious—these were not trained singers—and it was a shrewdly conceived gimmick that went over well. (He told one crowd in Toronto after singing with five beautiful women, "If I didn't have my job, I sure would want it.") In the end, the Because We Can tour became the biggest tour of 2013, grossing $260 million worldwide. It was the biggest set piece and tour the band had ever done.

Jon and Richie did not elaborate on the reasons for the latter's departure. Richie stated at the time that it was for personal reasons. Rumors about rehab, Richie being fired, and a feud were brushed off by both men. By late 2014, Jon acknowledged that Richie had left the band. The next year, Richie said he was leaving the door open for a return. Since 2013, both Jon and

PAGE 186: Jon Bon Jovi performing with the band at Gelora Bung Karno Stadium in Jakarta, Indonesia, September 11, 2015. It was the first of only nine overseas shows done in support of the album *Burning Bridges*.

OPPOSITE: Fresh-faced lead guitarist Philip Xenidis (aka Phil X) beams with enthusiasm during a Bon Jovi show at Soldier Field in Chicago, July 12, 2013.

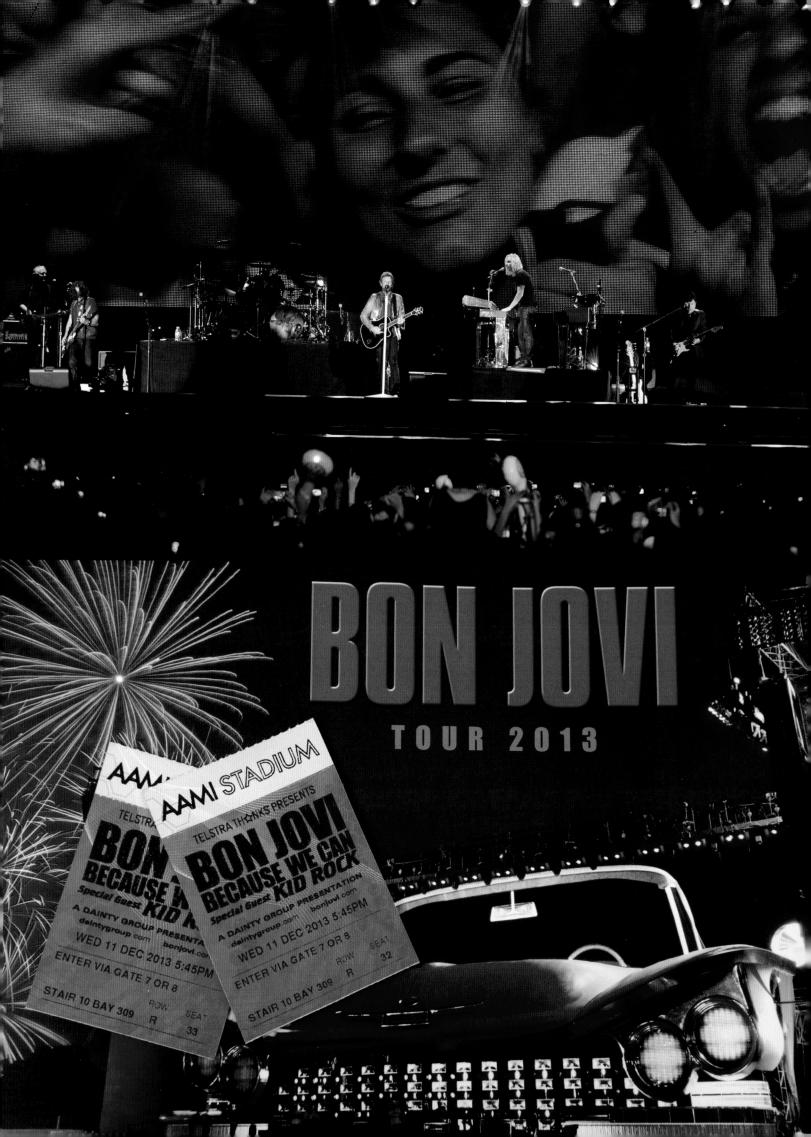

Richie have done numerous solo shows, and the singer has performed a number of charity concerts with his solo group the Kings of Suburbia. Violinist Lorenza Ponce often plays with him. Richie has been dating guitar wunderkind Orianthi and she has often played out live with him. It will be interesting to hear what music the duo crafts together. As of spring 2016, Bon Jovi and Richie Sambora were at work on new albums, Bon Jovi with John Shanks and Richie with Bob Rock. Of Richie's new album (possibly to be called *Rise*), Tommy Marolda says, "Bob did a great job. We wrote some great songs along with Orianthi and the new artist, Roman." Richie and Orianthi performed the song "This Town" with Roman at the Viper Room in Hollywood in April, and the couple teased their cover of the Sonny and Cher classic "I Got You Babe" last year. It will supposedly be on their forthcoming release. Bon Jovi's new album is tentatively slated as being called *This House Is Not for Sale*.

Although Richie has yet to release his next solo effort, there has been some new music from the Bon Jovi camp. To celebrate the thirtieth anniversary of *New Jersey* in 2014, the album was reissued as a double disc edition with a whole disc of the *Sons of Beaches* demos that did not make the final cut. The Super Deluxe Edition included DVD reissues of *New Jersey: The Videos* and the *Access All Areas: A Rock & Roll Odyssey* documentary released in 1990 and a sixty-page book with rare photographs and commentary. Then in 2015, Bon Jovi released *Burning Bridges*, which featured mostly unreleased material and two new cuts, "We Don't Run" and "Saturday Night Gave Me Sunday Morning," the latter co-written with Richie during the recording of *The Circle*. Meanwhile, on May 21, 2015, Jon received an honorary doctorate of letters from Rutger's University, where David Bryan had once studied. The singer wrote a song for the graduating throng called "Reunion."

Jon has called *Burning Bridges* a "fan album" but it was done to fulfill his contract to Mercury Records, which was his and the band's only home for thirty-two years. He was allegedly unhappy with the revolving door of executives at the Universal Music Group over the years. He had joked about that fact in a CNBC television interview with Tania Bryer in May 2012.

Considering it is essentially an album of castaways, *Burning Bridges* had its moments but was wildly inconsistent. The best tunes were the angsty lament "A Teardrop from the Sea," the upbeat "Saturday Night Gave Me Sunday Morning," the pretty ballad "Fingerprints," and the peppy yet sarcastic closing number; that folksy title track pretty much states the terms

A NEW ERA BEGINS

PAGES 190–91, TOP LEFT AND RIGHT: Fervent fans at the group's Rock In Rio concert in Rio de Janeiro, Brazil, on September 20, 2013. Women still love getting close to Jon.

PAGE 190, BOTTOM: A tour guide cover and tickets from Bon Jovi's tour stop in Adelaide, Australia, on December 12, 2013.

PAGE 191, BOTTOM: Jon sporting his Captain America-inspired denim jacket on a North Carolina tour stop on November 6, 2013. He wore it for many shows on the Because We Can tour.

"OBVIOUSLY BON JOVI'S MUSIC IS A BIG PART OF POP MUSIC CULTURE, AND ONE OF THE THINGS THAT REALLY IMPRESSES ME IS HOW LONG OF A RELEVANT CAREER THAT HE AND THE BAND HAVE HAD. I'LL GO ON TOUR SOMEWHERE AND SEE A POSTER FOR BON JOVI PLAYING SOME ARENA. HOW MANY BANDS ARE ABLE TO DO THAT FOR THAT LONG AND STILL HAVE THAT RELEVANCE AND SUPPORT? THAT'S UNBELIEVABLE."

John Petrucci, guitarist for Dream Theater, January 2016

OPPOSITE: Jon performs with his solo band the Kings of Suburbia at the Count Basie Theatre in Red Bank, New Jersey, on July 30, 2014. Most of his gigs since 2014 have been solo shows, the majority of them at charity galas.

that led to Bon Jovi's divorce from the only label he had ever been on. While not considered "new," it must have been written for this collection because of its specificity.

The band embarked on a limited number of tour dates overseas in 2015 to promote the album and their music, but they have not done any live dates in America since 2013. It remains to be seen, now that Richie is gone, how the songwriting of Bon Jovi will be affected. Phil X has played with his own raunchy hard rock band the Drills—they have songs like "I Wish My Beer Was as Cold as Your Heart" and "I Wanna Kill You Just a Little"—so he could inject a more vigorous guitar slant into their music, which would be good to hear again. It would also be great to have more contributions from David Bryan. The album cuts that the keyboardist co-wrote in the past—including "In These Arms," "Last Cigarette," and the B-side "Unbreakable"—have a larger-than-life quality to them and big choruses that are classic Bon Jovi.

An important aspect of Bon Jovi's career has been their ability to stay relevant by producing music that fans can still relate to. Their sets are only comprised of about one-third eighties tunes, the rest coming from the nineties onward. Entertainment reporter Cheryl Hoahing has noticed that American fans do not mind hearing the new songs. "It's got to be balanced—not just all new or all old," she observes. "They do a good mix, and I think Bon Jovi does that best. When AC/DC does a new song, everyone goes to get a beer. [With Bon Jovi] people still stay. I always joke with my friend that I'll go to the bathroom during 'Wanted Dead or Alive' because I've seen it 1,000 times. I don't need to see them do that again. I need to see a new song that's never been done before."

She adds that while fan reactions to Richie's departure have been mixed, "I don't think they've stopped listening," says Hoahing. "There are people out there on message boards who said they will never listen to Bon Jovi again, but for the most part they're okay. I think it will be interesting to hear the new music and see how the music changes, and that might reflect on Richie."

Jon's old bandmate Jack Ponti believes that the greatest band in the 1980s in terms of songwriting was Def Leppard—another band with a massive teen girl following that grew up with them. But the two bands have aged differently. "The reason why Leppard is not the size of Bon Jovi in 2016 is because when the older fans still look at Jon, he's aged so well, so gracefully, and so beautifully that they don't see their own mortality in him," believes Ponti. "I think that's the

A BRIEF HISTORY
OF HUGH

THE AGILE BASSIST WHO HAS PLAYED ON A MAJORITY OF BON JOVI'S ALBUMS, HUGH MCDONALD IS AN INDUSTRY VETERAN WHO WAS LANDING PRO GIGS WHEN JON AND RICHIE WERE STILL IN ELEMENTARY SCHOOL.

The sixty-five-year-old rocker hails from Philadelphia and has been a music lifer, lending his considerable talents to a wide swath of artists.

Starting in the late 1960s through the '70s, Hugh (known as Huey to his friends) recorded with a number of folk, roots, and country artists, including Willie Nelson, John Prine, Steve Goodman, and David Bromberg. By the 1980s, his repertoire expanded to include pop and rock artists like Lita Ford, Cher, Michael Bolton, Alice Cooper, and, of course, Bon Jovi. Since 1994, he has been the unofficial member of the Jersey Syndicate as Jon did not want to officially name a successor to original bassist Alec John Such.

However, Hugh is definitely a part of the band's DNA, and it helps that he loves the music. "I don't think there's any of the Bon Jovi songs that I get tired of playing," he told *iBass Magazine* in 2012. "I'm a fan first and foremost. I would listen to this stuff if I wasn't playing with the band."

A defining element of Hugh's bass work is his fluid style. He makes many difficult bass lines sound effortless, such as the funky parts in "Keep the Faith" or the grooving melodic lines of "Livin' on a Prayer." His pedigree from the folk and roots world undoubtedly has helped inform his rock performances, and he has become an indispensable part of the quintet.

Like guest violinist Lorenza Ponce, permanent if "unofficial" Bon Jovi bassist Hugh McDonald has gone on many adventures touring the globe with his musical buddies. "There are things that I have that are irreplaceable," McDonald told Scott Iwasaki of the Utah newspaper *Park Record* on September 13, 2013. "I have a Hofner violin bass that I had Paul McCartney sign and I had my picture taken with the Queen of England." He also got to stand on the coast of Africa many years ago with longtime Bon Jovi recording engineer and live mixer Obie O'Brien, whom he has been friends with going back to their early days in Philadelphia. "We stood at the edge of the continent, and looked at each other and said who would have guessed after all these years that we'd be here together. But the biggest reward about where my career has led me is meeting my wife Kelli."

In this case, the band gave love a good name.

OPPOSITE: Hugh McDonald has shied away from the limelight, despite being a longstanding feature of Bon Jovi's lineup. Here, the bassist is in action on December 19, 2005.

A NEW ERA BEGINS

❝ "AS LONG AS YOU'RE MAKING MUSIC THAT'S RELEVANT, YOU CAN BE HOWEVER OLD YOU WANT. B. B. KING SITS ON THAT STOOL EVERY NIGHT AND PLAYS; SINATRA SANG AND TOURED UNTIL HE WAS EIGHTY. I DON'T SEE ME DOING IT AT EIGHTY!" ❞

Jon Bon Jovi to journalist Talia Soghomonian, November 6, 2009

196 phenomenon of the longevity. That's not discounting the massive amount of work they put into touring because they did. I'm not discounting when they went to foreign territories when nobody else did because they did. That's not discounting Jon's work ethic because it's second to none."

Undoubtedly Jon's graceful aging, even with naturally graying hair that he chooses not to dye, has played a big factor in terms of his sex appeal. But the songs have a timeless quality to them that have reached out across multiple generations. Case in point: a Boston Celtics fan named Jeremy Fry was caught on camera lip syncing and dancing to "Livin' on a Prayer" back in 2009, high fiving and hugging crowd members while he danced awkwardly in the aisle. That joyful clip generated an even greater buzz in late 2013 when it began to be shared again across the internet (it has surpassed sixteen million views), and the result was that the song, buoyed by the YouTube clip which was shared over 1.6 million times in November 2013, reentered the Billboard Hot 100 at Number 25.

"Livin' on a Prayer" remains a staple of Bon Jovi shows. Unlike other aging rock stars who goad audiences into singing many lyrics to spare their voice, Jon only does it for this song since he knows that they will automatically sing the title line. And they relish doing it.

Beyond the classic hits, Bon Jovi have conjured up their fair share of modern singles that fans like, including "It's My Life," "Have a Nice Day," "Who Says You Can't Go Home" and "(You Want to) Make a Memory." The singer's insistence on moving ahead and not relying on past glories has spurred them to keep making new music. "He likes to talk about the present," says Glenn Gamboa, pop music critic for *Newsday*, who has interviewed the singer numerous times. "He has a desire to be liked by critics. He's really nice to critics because he believes that the band should be well regarded and he does what he can to have people look at him in a good light. He's a good guy. He loves talking about his charities and his work with Soul Kitchen."

Perhaps that elusive widespread acclaim will eventually come—not just from critics, but induction into the Rock 'n' Roll Hall of Fame, getting a Grammy for one of their rock tunes, and perhaps finally playing the halftime show at the Super Bowl. But that spirit of keeping in the moment has certainly allowed them to outlast trends and triumph while most of their eighties peers have found their fortunes dwindling since the nineties and have been relegated to nostalgia.

"I think the genius of the band and of Jon is that he is the only artist that was able to come from that world, in my opinion give birth to it, and be so incredibly associated with that

OPPOSITE TOP: Richie Sambora and Orianthi Panagaris share guitar duties during day one of the Calling Festival at Clapham Common in London, on June 28, 2014.

OPPOSITE BOTTOM: Rock legend Richie Sambora and country icon Dolly Parton rock the Pyramid Stage on day three of the Glastonbury Festival at Worthy Farm, Glastonbury, United Kingdom, June 29, 2014.

PAYING TRIBUTE

TRIBUTE BANDS ARE BIG BUSINESS THESE DAYS. FROM POP GROUPS TO HARD ROCKERS, MANY HIGH PROFILE MUSICIANS HAVE IN SOME CASES MULTIPLE CLONES PERFORMING THEIR MUSIC LIVE IN FRONT OF AUDIENCES EAGER TO HEAR THEIR TUNES, OFTEN FROM PARTICULAR PERIODS THAT ARE NOT LOOKED AT ANYMORE BY THE ORIGINAL ARTISTS THEMSELVES.

Bon Jovi have inspired a legion of tribute bands that are keeping the faith by playing both new and old hits. The band names easily tell people what they are about: Slippery When Wet, Bad Medicine, Bon Jersey, Bon Giovi, Wrong Jovi, Wanted, New Jersey, Livin' on a Prayer, even Blonde Jovi (an all-female version).

Tribute bands often try to emulate a particular time period of a famous band, especially those known for a big album or album cycle, so it is intriguing to note that none of the groups I found paying homage to Jon and the boys dress like Bon Jovi circa the 1980s, and essentially all of them dress as if it is 2000 or later. "I think for me it's because I found it to be more a believable tribute, not getting into the hokey '80s clothes," says Steve Sage, who has been the Jon of Long Island-based tribute band Bad Medicine since its inception in 2001. "The audiences that come see us want to hear Bon Jovi music, and I luckily resemble Bon Jovi. We have no need to do what the real band [did back then]." He adds that his tribute band has played songs all the way up to 2013's *What About Now*. They have toured America and in Ohio have drawn crowds of up to 9,000 people.

Clearly being in a tribute band is fun, and it can also generate some good business. Some of these bands play out several days a month. The venues can range from a local bar to a state fair or a cruise ship. Many of them elicit a strong crowd response since many Bon Jovi tunes inspire boisterous sing-alongs. And with a large catalog of songs to choose from, those groups paying homage to the Jersey quintet can change it up from gig to gig.

NYC-based eighties tribute band Rubix Kube regularly include a three-song Bon Jovi medley in their set, and fans expect "Livin' on a Prayer" to be a part of it. "It's amazing, it doesn't matter how many times we play 'Livin' on a Prayer,' people still go ballistic," Rubix Kube founder/singer Cherie Martorana tells me. "When we get to the Bon Jovi part of the show, I want to play so many different songs, but that one gets an insane reaction, and if we don't play it, people say, 'Why didn't you play "Prayer"?'" (Surprisingly, she notes that "Runaway" is not known by as many young fans, many of whom like it but have no idea who originally performed it unless told.)

Occasionally a tribute band gets lucky and draws the attention of official band members themselves. In 2002, Richie Sambora appeared onstage at the Canyon Club in Agoura Hills, California, to perform "Wanted Dead or Alive" with singer Bob Duda and *Slippery When Wet*. He played acoustic guitar and harmonized with the tribute vocalist. In 2015, David Bryan joined Rubix Kube onstage to rock out a medley of "Bad Medicine," "You Give Love a Bad Name," and "Livin' on a Prayer." He was all smiles and even came back out to help them do Journey's "Don't Stop Believin'." Years earlier, he joined Steel Panther/Metal Skool onstage to play "Runaway." He also covered "Wanted Dead or Alive" on a grand piano with classical pianist Elaine Kwon at Carnegie Hall in 2015 for a music education fundraiser. (They also rocked up "Chopsticks.") The two have performed together before, including at the Gershwin Hotel. (David is also loyal to his old Atlantic City Expressway bandmates, having appeared at past reunions.) The ultimate compliment was bestowed upon Long Island's Bad Medicine when they became the only

ONE WILD NIGHT OF GREATEST HITS, LIVE FAVOURITES & RARITIES

WRONG JOVI

"THE BEST BON JOVI TRIBUTE BAND IN THE WORLD!"
FACEBOOK.COM/WRONGJOVI   WRONGJOVI.COM   TWITTER.COM/WRONGJOVI

BON JERSEY
The Ultimate Bon Jovi Tribute Show

ABOVE: Promo images from tribute bands: Wrong Jovi and Bon Jersey.

tribute band to be approved by Jon to play for his AFL team, the Philadelphia Soul, while his brother Matt, who took over the fan club duties from their mother Carol, hired Steve Sage and Steve Frangadakas for a fan-club event celebrating Jon's fortieth birthday.

Despite the intense metalcore sounds of his band Atreyu, guitarist Dan Jacobs is a massive Bon Jovi fan. The group covered "You Give Love a Bad Name" for their half-a-million-selling album *The Curse* in 2004. Since then, the song has become a staple of their concerts. The guitarist says that they selected that anthem because they wanted to find a song they could adapt to their style, as he feels they have a pop sensibility beneath their aggressive exterior. "It gives at least one song that they can sing along to and be a part of the show," he notes, especially when new listeners "are completely disconnected by not knowing who you are or what's going on."

"There are people who don't know who Bon Jovi is and just know who we are, and they think that we wrote that song," admits Jacobs. "I wish I wrote that song. I'd be a lot more well off. Just the way that song starts off, with that big a cappella chant—as soon as we do that live, we don't even have to finish the line. Wherever we are in the world, the whole crowd finishes it for us. It's just an epic experience live."

❝ OUT OF ALL THE BANDS THAT YOU BECOME AWARE OF AS YOU TOUR THE WORLD, I HAVE TO SAY THAT BAND PROBABLY HAS GOT MORE PLATINUM AWARDS IN ALL PARTS OF THE WORLD THAN I'VE EVER SEEN. IT'S FREAKY. I'VE BEEN TO RADIO STATIONS IN NEW ZEALAND, INDIA, ITALY, YOU NAME IT, AND WHEREVER YOU GO YOU'RE GOING TO SEE A PLAQUE BY BON JOVI THAT SAYS SOMETHING UNHEARD OF. IF IT'S A SMALL COUNTRY, IT'LL SAY THIRTY-THREE TIMES PLATINUM. YOU'LL BE LIKE, WHAT?!? SO THEY DID SOMETHING RIGHT. ❞

Joe Satriani, legendary rock guitarist, February 2016

genre, yet [be] the only artist from an entire era to be able to completely reinvent themselves and now have no stigma from it whatsoever," says radio and TV personality Eddie Trunk. "Whether you like it or not, there is still a stigma associated with those bands from the eighties on MTV. . . . There are so many artists that you don't hear anything from that were huge on MTV back in those days. Bon Jovi is the one artist that completely reinvented [himself]. It's pretty masterful how he did that."

The question remains: where do both Jon and Richie go from here? It has been suggested that Jon will go solo for a while. Playing off the "Stand by Me" idea from a few years ago, perhaps he could do an album of duets with different singers. Or perhaps more philanthropy and political aspirations might be on the cards. While he has repeatedly expressed disdain for the idea of seeking political office, he has made friends with community leaders, senators, and presidents. He actually allowed New Jersey governor Chris Christie, a Republican, to use one of his songs during his failed presidential bid. Left-leaning artists of Jon's stature usually deny conservatives use of their songs in their campaigns since their messages are often at odds. His popularity and populist approach could play well in politics, despite his protestations against the possibility.

As for Richie, after his collaboration with Orianthi, there might be other musical vistas to explore. He could form a supergroup with some equally like-minded players and tour the world. For the City of Hope charity concert in 1996, he jammed onstage with John Mellencamp, Eddie Van Halen, Steve Winwood, Max Weinberg, and others. In 2015, he jammed onstage with Billy Gibbons, Slash, Steve Lukather, Duff McKagan, and Matt Sorum to raise money for Adopt the Arts. Perhaps more guitar duels await. When he was younger, Richie also expressed the desire to produce up-and-coming artists, which could still be a potential avenue for him.

"To me, the best thing that could have happened to Bon Jovi is for this whole thing to have gone on," asserts Sambora's longtime friend Bruce Foster when we speak. "Richie needed to experience his own life for a while. Since he was in his early twenties he's been in Bon Jovi. It's a corporation. He hasn't really had a chance to live his own life. Richie is just having a ball with his daughter, doing his thing, and being Richie Sambora. It's a wonderful, wonderful thing, and I think if they give it five or six years, if they give it ten years to get back together, it will be worth it."

OPPOSITE: Jon commands the stage at the Cotai Arena, Macao, China, September 25, 2015.

A NEW ERA BEGINS

DISCOGRAPHY

Note: Full track listings are detailed in album features throughout the book, so the below brief discography lists the certification details for each studio release.

STUDIO ALBUMS

Bon Jovi (January 1984) (for details, see p.42)
Producers: Tony Bongiovi; Lance Quinn
Labels: Mercury (US); Vertigo (Europe)
Certifications: Platinum (US); Gold (Canada, Switzerland); Silver (UK)

7800° Fahrenheit (April 1985) (for details, see p.50)
Producer: Lance Quinn
Labels: Mercury (US); Vertigo (Europe)
Certifications: Platinum (US, Canada); Silver (UK)

Slippery When Wet (August 1986) (for details, see p.59)
Labels: Mercury (US); Vertigo (Europe)
Certifications: Diamond (US, Canada); 6x Platinum (Australia); 3x Platinum (UK); 2x Platinum (Switzerland); Platinum (Finland, Germany, Spain); Gold (Hong Kong)

New Jersey (September 1988) (for details, see p.75)
Producer: Bruce Fairbairn
Labels: Mercury (US); Vertigo (Europe)
Certifications: 7x Platinum (US); 5x Platinum (Canada); 2x Platinum (Australia, UK); Platinum+Gold (Switzerland); Platinum (Austria, Finland, Germany, Spain)

Keep the Faith (November 1992) (for details, see p.104)
Producer: Bob Rock
Label: Mercury
Certifications: 5x Platinum (Canada); 3x Platinum (Australia, Switzerland); 2x Platinum (Austria, Japan, US); Platinum (Germany, Spain, Sweden, UK); Gold (Finland, France, Mexico)

These Days (June 1995) (for details, see p.115)
Producers: Peter Collins, Jon Bon Jovi, Richie Sambora
Label: Mercury
Certifications: Million (Japan); 4x Platinum (UK), 2x Platinum (Canada, Spain); Platinum (Australia, Austria, Finland, Netherlands, Switzerland, US); 2x Gold (France), Gold (Latvia, Germany)

Crush (June 2000) (for details, see p.141)
Producers: Luke Ebbin, Jon Bon Jovi, Richie Sambora
Label: Island
Certifications: 3x Platinum (Japan, Switzerland); 2x Platinum (Canada, Italy, Spain, US); Platinum (Argentina, Australia, Austria, Belgium, Finland, Mexico, UK); 5x Gold (Germany); Gold (France, Hungary, Poland, Sweden)

Bounce (October 2002) (for details, see p.146)
Producers: Luke Ebbin, Jon Bon Jovi, Richie Sambora
Label: Island
Certifications: Platinum (Canada, Germany, Japan, Switzerland); Gold (Argentina, Australia, Austria, Belgium, Brazil, Spain, UK, US)

Have a Nice Day (September 2005) (for details, see p.159)
Producers: John Shanks, Jon Bon Jovi, Richie Sambora, Rick Parashar, Dann Huff, Desmond Child (exec.)
Label: Island
Certifications: Platinum (Austria, Canada, Germany, Japan, Switzerland, US); Gold (Australia, Brazil, Greece, Spain, UK)

Lost Highway (June 2007) (for details, see p.162)
Producers: John Shanks, Dann Huff, Desmond Child (exec.)
Labels: Mercury Nashville; Island
Certifications: 3x Platinum (Canada); 2x Platinum (Austria); Platinum (Germany, Switzerland, US); Gold (Australia, Denmark, Hungary, Ireland, Japan, New Zealand, Spain, UK)

The Circle (November 2009) (for details, see p.175)
Producers: John Shanks, Jon Bon Jovi (co-producer), Richie Sambora (co-producer)
Label: Island
Certifications: Platinum (Canada); Gold (Australia, Germany, Japan, Switzerland, UK, US)

What About Now (March 2013) (for details, see p.181)
Producers: John Shanks, Jon Bon Jovi (co-producer), Richie Sambora (co-producer)
Label: Island
Certifications: Gold (Australia, Canada, Germany, UK)

Burning Bridges (August 2015)
Producers: John Shanks, Jon Bon Jovi (co-producer)
Label: Mercury
Top chart positions: 3 (UK), 13 (US, *Billboard*)
Track listings: 1. "A Teardrop to the Sea" (5:17); 2. "We Don't Run" (3:18) 3. "Saturday Night Gave Me Sunday Morning" (3:23); 4. "We All Fall Down" (4:05); 5. "Blind Love" (4:48); 6. "Who Would You Die for" (3:54); 7. "Fingerprints" (5:59); 8. "Life Is Beautiful" (3:22); 9. "I'm Your Man" (3:44); 10. "Burning Bridges" (2:44)

LIVE ALBUMS

One Wild Night Live 1985–2001 (May 2001)
Inside Out (November 2002)

COMPILATIONS

Hard & Hot (December 1991)

Cross Road (October 1994)

Tokyo Road: Best of Bon Jovi (March 2001)

This Left Feels Right (November 2003)

Greatest Hits (November 2010)

BOX SET

100,000,000 Bon Jovi Fans Can't Be Wrong (November 2004)

SPECIAL RELEASES/BONUS EDITIONS

Live on Tour EP (1987)

Live from Osaka (2000)

The Love Songs (2001)

Bon Jovi—Target® EP (2003)

Live from the Have a Nice Day Tour (2006)

SOLO ALBUMS

Jon Bon Jovi

Blaze of Glory (July 1990)

Destination Anywhere (June 1997)

Singles:

"Blaze of Glory" (1990), "Miracle" (1990), "Never Say Die" (1991), "Levon" (1992), "Please Come Home for Christmas" (1994), "Midnight in Chelsea" (1997), "Queen of New Orleans" (1997), "Janie, Don't Take Your Love to Town" (1997), "Ugly" (1998), "Everybody Hurts" (2010), "Not Running Anymore" (2012), "Love Song to the Earth" (2015), "Beautiful Day" (2015)

Live Albums:

At the Starland Ballroom Live (2009)

Compilation Albums:

John Bongiovi: The Power Station Years (1999)

The Power Station Years: The Unreleased Recordings (2001)

David Bryan

On a Full Moon (September 1995)

Lunar Eclipse (May 2000)

Richie Sambora

Stranger in This Town (September 1991)

Undiscovered Soul (February 1998)

Aftermath of the Lowdown (September 2012)

Singles:

"Ballad of Youth" (1991), "One Light Burning" (1991), "Stranger in This Town" (1991), "Mr. Bluesman" (1991), "Hard Times Come Easy" (1998), "In It for Love" (1998), "Undiscovered Soul" (1998), "Made in America" (1998), "Every Road Leads Home to You" (2012), "I'll Always Walk Beside You" (2012), "Sugar Daddy" (2012), "Come Back As Me" (2013)

SOURCES

INTERVIEWS WITH THE AUTHOR

Baronin, Vsevolod. January 21 and February 8, 2016.

Benabib, Roberto. February 3, 2016.

Bryan, David. March 2010.

Ebbin, Luke. January 12, 2016.

Fast, Larry. January 26, 2016.

Fiorello, Vinnie. January 21, 2016.

Fisch, Barry. January 12, 2016.

Flug, Gail. January 10, 2016.

Foster, Bruce Stephen. February 13 and March 31, 2016.

Frank, Bill. February 2, 2016.

Franco, Joe. February 2, 2016.

Gamboa, Glenn. January 28, 2016.

Giantonio, Laura. February 1, 2016.

Halford, Rob. January 12, 2016.

Hercek, Wil. February 22 and March 30, 2016.

Hoahing, Cheryl. January 9, 2016.

Jacobs, Dan. January 21, 2016.

Jolie, Rudd. January 17, 2016.

Karak, George. January 11 and February 12, 2016.

Kroeger, Mike. March 4, 2016.

Madadian, Andy. January 29, 2016.

Malluk, Eddie. January 7, 2016.

Marolda, Tommy. April 27, 2016.

Martorana, Cherie. February 15, 2016.

Miller, Gerri. December 16, 2015.

Mostow, Jonathan. February 22, 2016.

Petrucci, John. February 14, 2016.

Pierce, Tim. February 3, 2016.

Ponti, Jack. January 23 and 30, 2016.

Rarebell, Herman. February 7, 2016.

Ricci, Munsey. February 1, 2016.

Satriani, Joe. February 10, 2016.

Shirley, Kevin. January 23, 2016.

Shulman, Derek. February 3 and April 27, 2016.

Skolnick, Alex. January 30, 2016.

Smith, Billy. May 9, 2016.

Trunk, Eddie. January 5, 2016.

Workman, Lyle. January 18, 2016.

ADDITIONAL SOURCES
PRINT AND ONLINE

Abbot, Jim. "Bon Jovi Keeps the Faith, Stays True to His Roots," *Orlando Sentinel*, March 26, 1993.

Amendola, Billy. "Tico Torres of Bon Jovi." *Modern Drummer*, 2002.

Barber, Nicholas. "How We Met: Richie Sambora and Jon Bon Jovi." *Independent on Sunday*, January 7, 1995.

Benza, A.J. and Michael Lewittes. "Bon Jovi's Drummer A Gem." *New York Daily News,* November 5, 1996.

Bosso, Joe. "Production Legend Bob Rock on 16 Career-defining Records." *Music Radar*, March 1, 2013.

Connor, Cat. "The Interrogation of Lorenza Ponce!" CatConnorblogspot.com, November 19, 2010.

Dunham, Nancy. "Jon Bon Jovi: 'I Don't Live the Cliché, Rock Star Life'." *USA Today*, May 29, 2014.

DuNoyer, Paul. "The Jon Bon Jovi Interview." *Q magazine*, October 1997.

Iwasaki, Scott. "Bon Jovi Keyboardist Releases Instrumental, Non-rock Album." *Deseret News*, April 27, 2001.

Iwasaki, Scott. "Hugh McDonald Reflects on His Musical Career." *Park Record*, September 13, 2013.

"Jon Bon Jovi Gives His Home to Non-Jovi Judy Frappier." *People*, April 17, 1989.

Junior, Chris M. "A Shift in Style." *Medleyville.us*, February 1, 2011.

Leahey, Andrew. "Learning to Fly: A Q&A with Richie Sambora." *American Songwriter*, August 24, 2012.

Manzi, Peter. "David Bryan: Enjoying His Outlets, But Not Quitting His Day Job . . . and Why Would He?" *New Age Voice*, July 2001.

"My Life in Music: Kiefer Sutherland." *UNCUT magazine*, 2006.

Newton, Steve (earofnewt.com). "Jersey Boys Find a Home in B.C." *Georgia Straight*, November 18, 1993.

Newton, Steve (earofnewt.com). "Behind the Sounds." *Georgia Straight*, November 12, 1998.

Price, Deborah Evans. "Bon Jovi Puts a Jersey Spin on Country." *CMA Close Up News Service*, October 10, 2007.

Price, Deborah Evans. "Bon Jovi: Songwriting Duo Creates Hits for Others." *American Songwriter*, 1990.

Russell, Lisa. "New Jersey's Bon Jovi Runs Rings Around the Rock Competition with Its Slippery When Wet LP." *People*, November 24, 1986.

Selzer, Hal B. "Local Noise: Lorenza Ponce." *Aquarian Weekly*, May 26, 2010.

Simmons, Sylvie. Jon Bon Jovi Interview. *Request magazine*, 1996. Used with permission from the author.

Soghomonian, Talia. Interview with the Band. London, November 6, 2009. Used with permission from the author.

Tannebaum, Rob and Craig Marks. 2011. *I Want My MTV: The Uncensored Story of the Music Revolution*, New York: E. P. Dutton Co., Inc.

Tesoriero, Tobi Drucker. "The Music Man —David Bryan." *Living In Monmouth Magazine/Living In Media*, June 30, 2009.

Tingen, Paul. "Inside Track: Bon Jovi's *What About Now." Sound on Sound*, June 2013.

BROADCAST AND VIDEO

Desmond Child Special: The Welsh Show. April 2013

Inside The Actors Studio: Bon Jovi. Bravo Network. Original air date: November 16, 2009. Excerpts from *Inside the Actors Studio* © Actors Studio, Inc. Used with permission.

McCloud, Stacy. "Story Behind the Song: 'Livin' on a Prayer'." WZTV FOX 17, Nashville, March 22, 2013.

Nichols, Joe. *The Performers* series on Canadian TV. 1992.

Skepper, Catrina. Richie Sambora interview. *V.I.P.*, 1998. NBC Super Channel.

Thalo TV. Tico Torres Interview, January 2013.

Video Killed the Radio Star: Wayne Isham and Bon Jovi. Wayne Isham and Richie Sambora interviews, 2010.

PICTURE CREDITS

Key: t: top; b: bottom; l: left; r: right

Alamy: © AF Archive/Twentieth Century Fox: 127r; © AF Archive/Universal Pictures: 127bl; © AF Archive/Working Title Films: 127tl; © CBW: 59t, 75b; © Moviestore Collection: 89; © Pictorial Press Ltd.: 13 inset, 37; © Trinity Mirror/Mirrorpix: 123t; © WENN Ltd.: 109

Courtesy of Rich Antonelli: (www.bon-jersey.com): 199tr

Atlasicons: © Eddie Malluk: 24, 32/3, 38, 47, 54, 62 main, 70, 76, 78t, 78b, 79, 81, 99r, 100, 106t, 106b, 107t, 107b, 112/3, 154; © Neil Zlozower: 57

Cache Agency: (© Estate of Chuck Pulin): 53

Courtesy of Billy Falcon: © Mercury Records 95l;

Courtesy of Barry Fisch: 51r

Courtesy of Gail Flug: 61 © Mercury Records, 62 inset, 92r

Courtesy of Bruce Stephen Foster: 36r

Frank White Photography: © John T. Comerford III: 43; © Bob Leafe: 20; © Lynn McAfee: 35, 44/5; © Eleanor Reiche: 163; © Frank White: 15r, 17, 19r, 27r, 36l, 77, 195

Getty Images: © Vince Bucci: 69; © Jemal Countess/Songwriters Hall of Fame: 174; © Euroimagen Spain/Photoshot: 158; © Jeff Kravitz/FilmMagic Inc.: 97, 129, © Koh Hasebe/Shinko Music Archives: 7; © Richard Heathcote: 132; © Dave Hogan: 136, 143; © Franziska Krug: 118; © Larry Busacca Archive: 105; © LIFE Picture Collection: 75, 85, 110, 114; © Michael Loccisano/Getty Images for Tribeca Film Festival: 173; © Kevin Mazur: 86, 120, 124, 134, 135, 151, 177t, 177b, 151; © Jamie McCarthy: 13 main; © Michael Ochs Archives: 2, 23, 82, 123bl; © Michael Putland: 31; © Paul Natkin: 66, 67, 103; © Kelly Martin/Newsmakers: 139; © Ben A. Pruchnie: 197t; © Bill Pugliano: 169; © Brian Rasic: 3, 149; © Richard E. Aaron/Redferns: 14; © Samir Hussein/Redferns: 197b; © Mick Hutson/Redferns: 117; © Neil Lupin/Redferns: 9; © Martin Philbey/Redferns: 131; © Ebet Roberts/Redferns: 10; © Peter Still/Redferns: 165, 166, 167 main; © Agoes Rudianto /Anadolu Agency: 186; © Marcel Thomas: 125; © Rob Verhorst: 63; © Bruno Vincent: 147; © Theo Wargo: 150, 170; © Bobby Bank/Wireimage: 29, 192; © Stephen J. Cohen/Wireimage: 185; Rick Diamond/Wireimage: 160b; © Ron Galella/Wireimage: 91, 123br, 125; © Terry George/wireimage: 160tr; © Dimetrios Kambouris/Wireimage: 179; © John Medina/Wireimage: 160tl; © Lyle A. Waisman/Wireimage: 189

Courtesy of Laura Giantonio: 191l

Courtesy of Mark Harding: (www.wrongjovi.com): 199l, 199br

Courtesy of Wil Hercek: 15l

iStockphoto: © Lya Cattel: 145b; © CTR Photos: 190b

Courtesy of George Karak: 27l

The Kobal Collection (Full Moon Entertainment): 99l

Courtesy of Anne Lupin: 159b, 161, 162, 167 inset, 181b

Courtesy of Martin Popoff: 41

© Neal Preston: 90

Private Collection: 42, 49, 51l, 59, 65, 73, 92l, 95r © Mercury Records, 142, 153

Rex Shutterstock: © ImageChina: 201

Shutterstock: © Kyle Besler: 191b; © Steven Cashmore: 145t; © Featureflash Photo Agency: 157; © Netfalls—Remy Musser: 180; © Antonio Scorza: 183, 190t, 191t

AUTHOR BIOGRAPHY AND ACKNOWLEDGMENTS

A veteran entertainment journalist, **Bryan Reesman** has test driven a Corvette with Rob Halford, visited Lemmy's apartment, gone backstage with Cirque Du Soleil, and interviewed Oprah Winfrey. He has contributed to the *New York Times*, *Playboy*, *Grammy*, *American Way*, *MSN Movies*, and over a hundred other media outlets and written extensive liner notes for rock icons like Judas Priest, Black Sabbath, and AC/DC. Bryan has contributed to six books, including *The Art of Metal* (Voyageur), *Music Producers* (Hal Leonard), and *Classic Rock Posters* (Sterling). He is a graduate of New York University's Tisch School of the Arts. To read more about Bryan at www.bryanreesman.com.

The author would like to express heartfelt thanks to the following people for their valuable contributions:

My amazing editor Jo de Vries, who expertly guided me through my first book and showed tremendous patience and support for a project that ran on a very tight timeframe.

My wonderful photo editor Sally Claxton, who unearthed some fantastic pictures that greatly enhanced both the narrative and my research efforts.

Fellow rock journo Gail Flug whose invaluable input, insights, and images helped me further flesh out the story.

The candid Jack Ponti for intricately illuminating Jon's early years and connecting me with the helpful crew from the Fast Lane days—Laura Giantonio, Wil Hercek, Bill Frank, and New Jersey rock historian and collector, Billy Smith.

Thanks also to Barbara Berger at Sterling Publishing for championing the project and trusting my vision, the enthusiasm and input of Chris Thompson and Elizabeth Lindy from Sterling's design department, and the energetic efforts of Paul Palmer-Edwards at Grade Design in bringing the text and images to life.

Grateful thanks to Will Steeds and Laura Ward at Elephant Book Company for entrusting me with this project.

Lastly, a shout out to my family: my mother Maria, father Richard, and brother Eric.

I dedicate this book to them.

INDEX